A Taste of
HONEY

A Taste of HONEY

Honey for Health, Beauty & Cookery:
Recipes & Traditions

JANE CHARLTON &
JANE NEWDICK

CHARTWELL
BOOKS, INC.

A QUARTO BOOK

Published by Chartwell Books
A Division of Book Sales, Inc.
PO Box 7100
Edison, New Jersey 08818-7100

This edition for sale in the U.S.A., its territories
and dependencies only.

ISBN 0-7858-0349-1
This book was designed and produced by
Quarto Publishing Plc
The Old Brewery
6 Blundell Street
London N7 9BH

Art Director: Moira Clinch
Design: Design Revolution
Senior Art Editor: Liz Brown
Copy Editors: Jackie Matthews and Fiona Hunter
Home Economist: Jane Charlton
Picture Researcher: Jo Carlill
Picture Manager: Giulia Hetherington
Senior Editor: Sian Parkhouse
Editorial Director: Mark Dartford
Photographer: David Sherwin
Illustrators: Fred Van Deelen, Elizabeth Dowel

Typeset in Great Britain by Central Southern Typesetters, Eastbourne
Manufactured in Hong Kong by Regent Publishing Services Ltd
Printed in China by Leefung-Asco Printers Ltd

Contents

INTRODUCTION

Honey has been sought after for centuries. In the past a taste of this amber elixir could placate the gods, arouse feelings of love, and inspire great cooks. And the unique flavor of this sweet substance still guarantees it a place in the affections and pantry cupboards of people today.

Aristotle, one of the earliest believers in honey's efficacy

Spiced bread, flavored with honey.

Honey has inspired many fascinating legends; stories of its magical powers have been passed down through history. People of ancient civilizations realized the value of honey and came up with innovative ways to use it, both as a foodstuff and in other, more esoteric, ways. Pharaohs were sent off to their eternal journey to the after-life with pots of honey, and the enterprising Egyptians also discovered that honey was an excellent medium for embalming their dead.

Great philosophers and physicians, such as Aristotle and Hippocrates were fascinated by the industrious bees. They captured them in hives, studying their complex communities and harvesting the honey for their own consumption.

Astutely recognizing both honey's healing power and therapeutic qualities, the Greeks and Romans soon transported the pot of honey from the table to the physician's surgery. Many of the remedies they devised are still used to promote health, vitality, and long life today – using their recipes we can still make them.

Honey was also seized upon for its cosmetic applications. Legendary beauties such as Cleopatra and Madame Du Barry are among the countless women through the centuries who have included honey in beauty preparations for its purifying and enhancing qualities, and modern women can also benefit from it, both in commercial creams and homemade treatments.

Of course, these potions and lotions would

Beekeeping has an old and venerable tradition, as is demonstrated in this fifteenth-century manuscript.

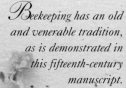

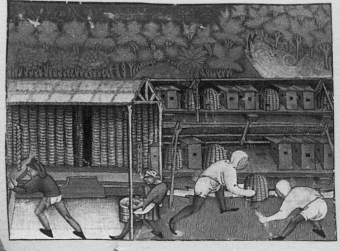

not exist without the resourceful bee, traveling from blossom to blossom collecting nectar from different flowers and turning it into the treasured golden substance by a process akin to alchemy. We have harnessed this magical skill through beekeeping, and we can now choose from countless varieties of honey from all over the world. Each has its own distinctive flavor and scent: discover reosemary honey from the Mediterranean, eucalyptus honey from Australia, tupelo honey from the United States, and lavender honey from France.

We all relish the tastes of honey can bring to everyday foods – toast and honey, for example is a staple from childhood. But historical recipes divulge some more unusual combinations. The famous gourmet Apicius created a whole banquet from dishes prepared with honey.

While we may not find his more exotic recipes very appetizing, such as honey-baked tortoise or peacock in honey sauce, we can be inspired by his inventiveness. Honey adds a certain richness of both color and taste to a variety of foods, both savory and sweet – simple snacks for any time of the day, honeyed meats and poultry, luscious desserts, scrumptious cakes, and tempting drinks.

Souvenir International Health Exhibition. 1884.

Presented by F. Allen & Sons.

Manufacturers of Cocoa, Chocolate and Confectionery

"Sweetness & Health"

City House, Bishopsgate Street. E.C.   Works. Canal Rᵈ Mile End. London

7

With such diverse uses, it is not surprising that honey is as popular as ever, and many more people are discovering why it was indispensable to ancient civilizations. Honey today is appreciated as an unadulterated, natural product, less processed than any other sweetening agent, and with fewer calories. It is now a major commodity, with a total of nearly a million tons produced worldwide every year.

The honey bee has long been associated with health and well being, so it is easy to see why the organizers of the International Health Exhibition in 1884 should have chosen it as their symbol.

A traditional wooden honey drizzle, used to pour thin streams of honey.

This lid from a jar of blended honey carries the trademark bear of The Bear Honey Company, an animal long associated with honey.

THE STORY OF THE BEE

REMAINS OF PRIMITIVE BEE-LIKE INSECTS HAVE BEEN FOUND ENCAPSULATED IN BALTIC AMBER FROM THE EOCENE PERIOD, SOME 50 MILLION YEARS AGO. THEY SLOWLY EVOLVED INTO THE CREATURES WE KNOW TODAY AS HONEYBEES.

A fifteenth-century illustration of a bee from a manuscript with text around it. Very little attempt has been made to draw the insect in an anatomically correct way, but the little image of the bee makes a strong and colorful motif.

The domestic honeybee we have today belongs to the race *apis mellifera*. Linnaeus classified it as *mellifera* (honey-bearing), then changed it to *mellifica* (honey-making) after discovering that the insects made honey in the hive, rather than collecting it. Today there are four species of *apis* in the world, which all build wax combs and store a surplus of nectar and pollen. Before man introduced the domestic bee to different countries, *apis mellifera* was found only in Europe and Africa, and there were no honey bee species native to North and South America, New Zealand, Australia, New Guinea, or the South Pacific islands.

In effect, there is a class structure of bees, with each one having a specific purpose within the colony. The size of a colony of bees can vary enormously, but on average at peak population periods, a hive or nest may contain 30,000 to 40,000 worker bees, one queen, and 500 to 1,000 drones. In winter in temperate climates, this figure will be reduced to a queen and about 500 to 12,000 workers.

The queen is the matriarch of the colony, and she will live for three to four years. Generally, there is only one breeding queen in a hive. She begins life by being reared in a special queen cell in the wax comb, hatching from an egg laid by the previous queen, who will be replaced by her. She is fed by worker bees on a diet of royal jelly and carefully nurtured, licked clean, and generally pampered until in sixteen days she is fully grown. Several queens may be raised at the same time, but most will be stung to death, while others may leave with swarms.

THE MATING GAME
The queen will mate with the male drone bees. After mating, the queen should have five million sperm stored so that she can begin laying eggs in the brood nest. She will continue to do so through the spring and summer and right up to the winter, when she stops, before resuming again the following spring. She lays fertilized eggs which will become workers in some cells; and in other, larger cells she lays unfertilized eggs which will become the male drones.

A foraging honeybee with full pollen sacs working among apple blossoms in an orchard in late spring. Tree blossoms make up a large part of the plants visited by worker bees.

The female workers in a hive do everything required to keep the colony functioning. In busy times of year, such as the height of summer, they may live for only six weeks. Once hatched, the new workers will be given a sequence of work, starting with cleaning and caring for the nursery quarters, then feeding the larvae. At six to ten days old, they will take their first flights outside. Next they start to secrete wax and build new wax cells, then move on to receiving and storing the nectar. At two to three weeks old, they progress to entrance guarding and fanning their wings to keep the hive cool and clearing away debris. Only then do they begin to fly from the hive to collect nectar, pollen, and propolis, a glue-like substance taken from sticky buds and leaves.

BUSY BEES

Foraging is what really exhausts the worker bee, taking her up to 3 miles from the hive at a time. The bee will suck nectar from deep inside the flower and store it in her honey sac, picking up pollen as she moves among the flowers and storing this on her back pair of legs. The journey back to the hive is by the shortest and quickest route (hence the term "making a beeline for.") and once home, the nectar and pollen are taken by another worker or put by her into cells. It takes between 20,000 and 100,000 journeys to bring a litre of nectar back to the hive.

One fascinating aspect of the worker bee's life which has been studied carefully over the years is the means of communication between the bees by means of "dance." For example, at the beginning of the year when the first workers go off searching for nectar, they need to let the other workers know when they have found it. This is done by performing several different and distinct dances which describe just where the nectar source is and how far away it is. In the 1920s the Bavarian bee expert Professor Karl Ritter von Frisch isolated and identified some of these, which have come to be known as the Round dance, the Wagtail dance, and the Sickle dance.

THE DRONES

Virgil described the drones in a hive as "that pack of shirkers" whose main purpose is to mate with the queen. The drone is larger than a female worker, weighing about the same as a queen, and with distinctive large compound eyes meeting on the top of the head. Probably only a very few of the hundred males will mate with the queen, and at the end of the summer the surplus drones are chased from the hive and harassed until they fly away. Unable to forage for themselves, they soon die of starvation.

Australian worker bees and their queen on a section of comb in a hive used for pollen storage.

9

THE QUEEN

The queen's body is elongated and her wings extend only part of the way back over her abdomen. Her legs are long, with no pollen-collecting sacs, and her stinger is curved.

THE DRONE

The drone weighs about the same as a queen and has large wings which cover the blunt abdomen. The thorax is quite square, and the large compound eyes almost meet.

THE WORKER

The worker is half the weight of a drone or queen, with a hairy body and straight stinger. The wings almost cover the abdomen and the legs have pollen- collecting apparatus on them.

Bees and their Beehives

Since humans first took bees from the wild and began beekeeping, hive design has evolved differently all over the world.

An elaborate European garden design from the 1820s shows how beekeeping fitted into what was becoming a more formal landscape style. Siting the bee shelter by the pool fulfilled two functions: it complemented the overall design, and also made it easy to get to the hives.

Before people learned how to keep bees in artificial hives, honey was collected from the wild, often destroying the bees and their nests in the process. The honey bee's natural habitat of a hollow tree was sometimes removed to a settlement by sawing it into a portable size and setting it up as an early version of domestic beehive. Even then, the bees were generally sacrificed for the honey. The early Egyptians learned how to breed bees in artificial nests or hives made from interwoven twigs and reeds and baked mud. These were shaped like long cylinders and stacked together horizontally with the gaps between them filled with clay. Both the Greeks and Romans used cylindrical hives, made not only from clay, but of many different materials such as woven wattle, dung, cork bark, wood, or logs. Horizontal hives are still used in many less-developed areas of the world today, such as parts of Africa and South America.

THE ALVEARY

The first vertical hives date back to between 100 and 500 A.D. The problem with keeping bees in this way was how to extract the honeycomb, which was not as simple as removing it from horizontal hives. The usual method was to destroy the bees with sulfur fumes, or by drowning, to get at the comb, leaving just a few colonies to overwinter. The earliest types of hive were made from woven wicker, and the remains of one of these have been dated at around 200 A.D. This simple kind of hive, sometimes known as an "alveary," was conical in shape and made from woven willow or hazel, like a tall, pointed, upturned basket. The structure was covered both inside and out in cloam (a soft daub made from lime and animal dung which hardened into a waterproof coating, keeping the bees safe and dry inside). A "hackle" or bunch of straw, was pushed over the top of the hive to divert the rain from the sides. Examples of this type of hive were still being used up to 1885.

THE STRAW SKEP

Straw "skeps" were made possibly as early as the beginning of the Christian era – in parts of western Europe and became widespread throughout the whole of the continent. The origin of their name is puzzling. Some scholars argue that it comes from the Norse word *skeppa*, meaning a container or measure for grain, but it is known

A Mr. Saul wrote to the Mechanics Magazine in 1829 with this design for his Improved bee-house. It was designed so that the house could be turned so that the entrance was always away from the wind (which must have confused the bees no end); hence the weather vane on top. It also had a device for measuring the weight of the hive, and therefore the honey. Inside was a straw hive, but the outer construction would appear to be aimed at pleasing bishops or priests rather than mechanics.

that the word skep did not come into common use until about the sixteenth century. In Britain skeps were still being used up to the nineteenth century, even alongside modern wooden hives, and they are still used today by some beekeepers to collect swarms. The advantages of the straw skep were that the materials were cheap and few tools were needed to make it. Straw was the most common material, but in areas where it was scarce, reed might be used, or – in uplands with little arable land purple moor grass. The straw was pushed through a hollow bone or cow's horn to form

The thick walls of this Devonshire house are deep enough to have a couple of boles cut into them to house bee "skeps," although placed where they are, reaching them must have been difficult.

This elegant hive on a pole comes from a period, probably the early nineteenth century, when all kinds of experimental hive shapes were being developed.

tight rolls, which were then coiled spirally and bound together neatly with strong lengths of bramble stem. Skeps evolved and changed shape over the years, becoming flatter rather than conical so that several could be stacked together. Their main disadvantage was that the straw could rot in a wet season, which meant providing some kind of additional shelter.

BEE BOLES AND HOUSES

A "bee bole" was a niche, or alcove, in a house or garden wall where straw skeps could be kept out of the worst weather. In their most primitive form, the boles were often no more than spaces left in a dry stone wall, but in grander gardens and estates, they were often built with care and attention to detail. At Packwood House in Warwickshire, England, the garden wall has a series of 30 bee boles cut into it. Boles were most common in England and Ireland where they were extensively used in the seventeenth and eighteenth centuries. In hotter countries such as Spain and parts of North Africa, bee walls – stacks of horizontal hives kept permanently in a long wall – were more common. In Germany, bee houses were used to keep multiple colonies of bees together. These were sometimes very elaborate permanent buildings made of wood or stone, with the hives facing out in all directions and room inside for the beekeeper to work and get at the hives. This type of bee house spread to eastern Europe, where Austria, Poland, Bohemia, and Slovakia all had fine examples of these

A traditional bell-shaped straw skep from the 1840s.

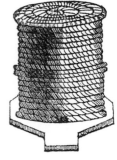

Wildman's storyed straw beehive with wooden spars at the top on which the bees could build the comb.

A Grecian or Candiote straw hive with wooden spars for the comb.

buildings. A few grand country houses in England had specially made bee houses, often in a style of architecture to complement or match the main house itself. Though practical, they were also important as part of the overall design of the garden and the environs of the house.

MODERN HIVES

As beekeeping developed, it became clear that it was no longer acceptable to destroy colonies to get honey or to rob skeps of all the comb, so that the bees starved during the winter. Experiments were carried out to try to make suitable hives which protected the bees and simplified the removal process. By the mid-seventeenth century, skeps were "storified," or stacked together, meaning that a box of combs could be removed without killing the colony. Various systems were devised to separate the bees when necessary and to isolate the honeycomb for removal. Professional and amateur beekeepers experimented during the

From this colony of bees in a hollow tree, it is easy to see how the bees construct their comb without human interference. The bees simply fill the available space, and so the wax structure is quite free-form.

13

This is an Indian pot hive made from earthenware and propped horizontally in the crook of some tree branches. This style of hive was common throughout the ancient world and is still used today.

This is a replica of the earliest kind of wattle and daub hive or alveary. The willow twigs are not totally covered, so it is possible to see how they are woven. The whole design has a pleasing, almost organic form.

Two styles of nineteenth-century wooden beehives, one simple and the other quite grand, and a traditional straw skep on a stand and with a straw cover.

A female beekeeper works in her apiary of wooden hives in Lismore, Ireland, in 1890. She is smoking one hive with bellows and seems ready to collect some honey with a bowl and spoon.

14

latter half of the eighteenth century and the first half of the nineteenth, and the concept of removable frames became established. These frames could be built upon by the bee and easily removed, but the problem of the bees building between the frames and gluing them together remained unsolved.

The real breakthrough came in 1851, when the Reverend Lorenzo Lorraine Langstroth from Pennsylvania discovered "bee space." This was the space needed between the parts of a hive which was too big for the bee to fill with comb, but left enough room for the insects to move around freely. The Langstroth hive has been the model for most subsequent hives with the WBC, modern Langstroth, and "National Hive Design" all based on the same principal. In 1857, a German named Mehring had the

A print published in London in 1851 shows an example of Pettitt's Temple beehive. On the left it is closed, and on the right we can see (A) the feeding drawer, (B) the brood hive, and (C) two glass hives to be added when (B) is nearly full of comb.

Examples of eighteenth-century hives from Hungary carved from tree trunks and based on the most primitive forms of early hives.

brilliant idea of making sheets of beeswax, imprinted with the hexagonal cell shape, which were fitted into the frames ready for the bees to build out from. These sheets of wax are known as foundation and are familiar as the material used for rolled beeswax candles. At roughly the same time, Abbé Collin in France invented the queen excluder – a sheet of perforated metal used in the hive to keep the queen in the nursery quarters and from laying in the upper chambers of the hive. The workers can move through it and deposit nectar above the queen and then frames full of honey can be removed without disturbing the bees.

BARCS

For centuries, in densely forested parts of eastern Europe, people kept bees in "barcs," or hollowed-out trees. This method was still used up to the 1930s, and it made good sense in these areas where trees were the bees' natural habitat. Beekeepers selected old, wide-girthed trees and made one or more cavities, usually about 3 yards from the ground, but sometimes up to 20 yards above. A special board was positioned at the entrance to the barc, and a log was left to swing in front of the cavity to deter bears from robbing the nest. Honey was harvested once a year, after the honey flow had finished.

A straw hive in France, dating from the 1890s or early 1900s, with an extra topknot to protect it from the sun and a tile to keep the rain out.

Experiments have been done to find which color is best for a beehive. Traditionally they were often painted white, but pastel colors such as pale sky blue seem effective for the bee to locate its base easily.

In former Yugoslavia, elaborate bee houses were very common, holding several colonies at a time. This is a hive on a smaller scale in the bee museum at Radorljica; it is designed as a miniature house, though the complicated decoration makes it hard to see how it worked as a hive for bees.

15

A quite extraordinary wooden beehive made in the shape of a man, with the entrance for the bees above his belt and between his legs. It is in a bee museum in Croatia.

From The Hive to The Honey Pot

BEEKEEPERS HAVE ALWAYS BEEN SEEN AS SOMEWHAT SPECIAL PEOPLE AND HELD IN GREAT RESPECT, PARTICULARLY BY THOSE WHO KNOW LITTLE ABOUT BEES AND SEE THEM ONLY AS A TERRIFYING, STINGING MASS. IN ANCIENT TIMES BEEKEEPERS WERE REVERED AND HELD IN HIGH ESTEEM, THEIR KNOWLEDGE AND PATIENCE CONSIDERED IMPORTANT AND EVEN PROFOUND. LUCKILY FOR ALL OF US WHO LOVE HONEY, BEEKEEPING IS STILL ALIVE AND WELL.

There is no doubt that the first steps to good beekeeping are to learn about and understand the creatures you are dealing with and the natural world they inhabit. From then on, beekeeping is just like any other area of animal husbandry, all of which demand regular care and maintenance, time, skill, and experience gained over the years. What makes bees different from many other creatures is that they remain wild insects. While we may make use of them, we must remember that they do not need us.

Getting honey from the hive to the honey pot will take a year of good management. On the first fine, warm day of the year, the bees will emerge from the hive on a "cleansing flight" and begin to search for early nectar- and pollen-producing plants. Soon after, the beekeeper will inspect the hive for any winter damage and assess how strong the colony is. The queen should have started laying eggs in the brood cells, and there should still be enough food left for the workers. Beekeepers use a smoker to calm the bees to make inspection easier. The smoke causes the bees to become drowsy and less aggressive.

The Critical Time

A month or so later, the egg cells should be well-stocked with eggs and larvae and plenty of "bee bread" or honey and pollen stocks. Extra honey may be provided as food and water if needed, and new frames inserted with fresh new wax foundation in place. Old debris and trash will be cleared away and re-queening done if necessary. The next few weeks may be critical if the weather suddenly turns cold, so the beekeeper watches and checks that the workers have been collecting enough food for all the newborn bees. By late spring the hive may swarm, which can mean a lot of work for the beekeeper. A swarm happens when most, or all, of a hive take off at once following the old queen. It is not completely clear why a colony swarms, but it may be because they are running out of room, or it is too hot inside the hive, or it may be nature's way of preventing disease by moving home. One main swarm will generally be followed by several more, depending on how many young queens are left in the hive. The beekeeper will collect the swarm as soon as possible from its first stopping point, which is often on a branch of a tree, before the swarm can move on to a cavity or a more inaccessible final destination. Swarms give the beekeeper a good chance of starting a fresh hive or building up a weak colony.

Harvesting the Rewards

By early summer, the honey should be building up and all should be well with the bees. Hives can be moved through the season to catch a particular crop. Examples of this are hives moved into orchards for the tree blossom (a move which also helps the growers with fruit

A WBC hive (named after William Broughton Carr, who invented it early this century) stacked high with layers called supers, promising a large crop of honey later in the summer. The lowest super is the brood box, and the four above it are for honey storage. Four of these is about the maximum to expect in one season.

16

1 *This double-walled WBC hive is very active with foraging bees. Twenty-four hours before taking honey the keeper puts a clearing board in place to stop bees from going up into the super he wishes to extract.*

This is a simple type of bee hat with black veil. Though mostly superseded by zip-on versions which can be attached to a boiler suit, this version is cheap and fairly effective – as long as the ties are tight!

2 *The bees will know the honey is being taken and may get angry. It is essential to wear protective clothing, especially a hat and veil, which then gives the bee-keeper the confidence to work easily and smoothly. First the lid is lifted off.*

fertilization) or to moorlands for the heather flowers.

Oilseed rape honey has to be taken from the hive very soon after it has been collected, as it sets hard in the comb if left too long. Otherwise, the main honey harvest is usually later in the summer when the heavy frames are taken from the hive and the capping, or layer of wax sealing in the honey to each cell, is removed with a hot knife. Honey is generally taken from the frames by spinning the wax in a centrifugal extractor. It is then filtered and bottled. The wax may be cleaned and melted down for all kinds of other uses. A typical hive could yield up to 90 pounds of honey, depending on the season and the strength of the colony. In England August 24 or the feast of St. Bartholomew, is the latest date for taking honey. From then on, the beekeeper checks his colonies, takes any action needed against disease, and by early autumn starts to feed the bees with a sugar or honey solution. This gives them enough time to build stocks of honey for themselves through the winter months. The upper chambers are removed from the hive to concentrate the insects into a smaller space.

3 *Inside, the frames the bees have filled are exposed; you can see that a few stray bees are still present. Smoke is puffed into the hive, which will keep the bees calm and less likely to attack. The bees on the frame can be brushed gently away; traditionally this is done with a goose feather.*

18

Smokers have not changed much in design over the years. Basically they consist of a chamber, which holds something combustible such as dry grass, corrugated cardboard, or old burlap sacks, and bellows to force the smoke through the funnel.

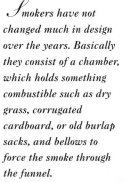

4 *Next the frames are lifted out and checked for honey. They are surprisingly heavy when full. Frames which are going to be harvested are taken indoors to a bee-tight room in case the insects follow. Before extracting honey, the hive should be closed again and left in order.*

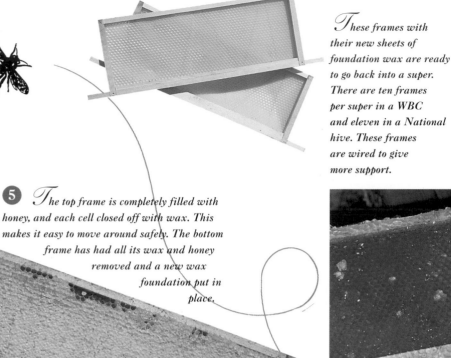

These frames with their new sheets of foundation wax are ready to go back into a super. There are ten frames per super in a WBC and eleven in a National hive. These frames are wired to give more support.

5 *The top frame is completely filled with honey, and each cell closed off with wax. This makes it easy to move around safely. The bottom frame has had all its wax and honey removed and a new wax foundation put in place.*

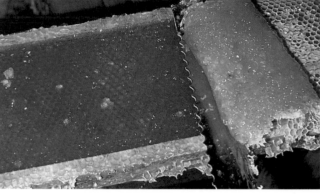

6 *The wax capping covering the comb is scraped off evenly to expose the liquid honey. A long-bladed knife is best for this. Then the frames are scraped or spun to remove the honey, which is usually filtered before bottling.*

19

A galvanized metal honey extractor from the very early part of this century. Hand-cranked machines have altered very little, though now they tend to be made from plastic. A machine like this would take up to four frames at a time.

Examples of clear liquid honey. The darker one is a tree blossom honey and the paler one a mixed wildflower honey. Both are crystal clear and runny, but in time will crystallize naturally unless they are treated.

THE STORY OF HONEY

HONEY AND BEES ARE MENTIONED AS FAR BACK IN TIME
AS WE ARE ABLE TO GO. THE HISTORY OF HONEY IS A FASCINATING EXPLORATION
COVERING EVERY ASPECT OF HUMAN LIFE.

Representations of bees figured frequently in Egyptian hieroglyphs. These appear on an obelisk at the temple of Karnak.

Plutarch, the celebrated Greek biographer and philosopher, who traveled the length and breadth of Britain in the second century A.D., remarked that "These Britons only begin to grow old at 120 years of age" and connected their long life to the amount of mead they drank.

The date when man enjoyed his first taste of honey is not known – we can only surmise that the earliest hunter–gatherers must have come across a wild bees' nest in a hollow tree or bank of soil and plundered it. A few bee stings would be quickly forgotten, but the sweetness of the honey would remain in the memory, in contrast to their normally unpalatable diet of game, plants, and nuts.

The Neolithic revolution, when man progressed from hunting to farming and stockbreeding, was a slow business and happened at different speeds in various parts of the world. As the glaciers receded, from around 12,000 B.C., the climate gradually warmed up, resulting in the widespread colonisation of fast-growing plants, such as wild grains. Settlements were built near these plentiful wild crops, and it slowly became clear that some seeds could be retained from one harvest and sown to produce another.

Around the same time, animals began to be herded and domesticated; and, wherever the conditions were right, bees were taken from the wild and kept in primitive hives to provide honey and beeswax. The earliest illustration we have of honey being gathered is in a wall painting around 15,000 years old, which appears on the walls of rock shelter in eastern Spain.

It is thought that the nomadic people of central Asia may have introduced honey to the world, as many of its early names seem to have similar origins. The Sanskrit word *madhu*

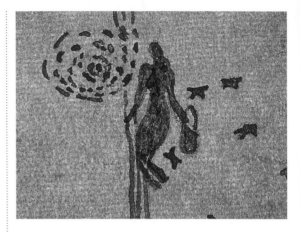

In this prehistoric wall painting, a female figure appears to have angered the bees in her attempt to extract honey.

and the Chinese *myit* have echoes in the Slav word *medhu* and the English word *mead*.

THE EGYPTIANS AND GREEKS

Honey was a vital commodity for the ancient Egyptians, who used it as a food, as an offering to their gods, and as an ingredient in embalming fluids. During the First Dynasty in Lower Egypt, around 320 B.C., the bee became the symbol of the pharaoh and was used to represent his kingdom. From then on, the bee was regularly used to symbolise royalty in the hieroglyphs of the time. It is not hard to understand how people felt about the bee and its capacity to create something in such quantity from very little. In the days before biology and botany were understood, people must have

thought it was a special kind of magic which turned flower nectar into honey.

The Egyptians kept their bees in tall, cylindrical hives: similar hives of this type are still used in remote parts of Egypt today. The honey was collected by smoking one end of the cylinder to drive the bees to the opposite one, a method illustrated in tomb reliefs from this period. About half the honeycomb was then removed and the bees left alone again.

Beeswax was also of great importance – it was used for cosmetics and embalming as well as for writing tablets and encaustic painting: a method whereby pigments and resins were added to molten, bleached wax, which was then applied with a knife to a suitable surface. Heat was applied to set the colors and make the paint permanent. Encaustic painting was much used by the Egyptians, particularly for decorating the life-size portrait of the face on wood which was laid on the face of a mummy. The Egyptians

sometimes paid taxes in honey, and beekeepers were taxed on their bounty. Great quantities of it were used as sacrifices, gifts to the gods, and as grave goods to accompany kings to the afterlife. Records show that in the twelfth century B.C., the king of Egypt, Rameses III, sacrificed 15 tons of honey to the Nile god Hapi – a staggering amount. Honey was also baked into special honey cakes, which were used as offering to placate the gods throughout ancient Egypt. A painted relief from the tomb of Rekh-mi-re, built around 1450 B.C., shows a line of Egyptian bakers making the cakes and putting them in a clay oven. Some uneaten cakes from this period have been found, but how effective they were at pleasing the gods, we shall never know!

The Greeks also made little honey cakes from flour, honey, and oil, sometimes baked with fresh flowers inside them, as supplications to their gods. They considered honey to be an

Honey was a vital commodity in Egyptian culture and commerce. This papyrus from 1258 B.C. shows Ani, a scribe, and his wife Tutu making an offering to the god Osiris which would certainly have contained honey.

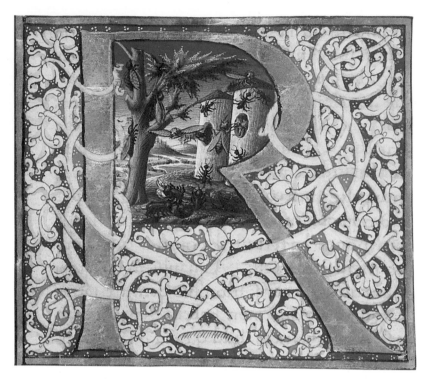

Pliny the Elder wrote at length about bees in Historia Naturalis, *from which this illuminated initial, showing a beehive besieged by ants, is taken.*

22

The Romans loved honey and used it extensively in cooking. This pavement mosaic from the first century shows a typical banquet.

important food as well as a healing medicine; Greek recipe books of the time seemed to abound with all kinds of irresistible sweetmeats and cakes made from honey. Goat or sheep milk cheeses were mixed with it to make cheesecakes, described by Euripides in the fifth century B.C. as being "steeped most thoroughly in the rich honey of the golden bee."

There are numerous pieces of Greek literature on the subject, such as this early one from Hesiod, writing in 700 B.C.: "Every day the bees work eagerly all throughout the day till sundown and set the white combs, while the drones stay within the roofed hives and gather into their bellies the toils of others." Beekeeping was seen as a noble and worthwhile pastime, and the keeping of bees was widespread among rich and poor.

WHEN IN ROME

Later, in ancient Rome, hives were made from all kinds of substances. Pliny writes about the various merits of different materials, including bark, fennel plant, and withies (willow twigs). He also describes a transparent material, believed to have been mica, used in hives so that the workings of the bees could be seen from the outside. Other materials included cork, logs, dung, brick, wood, and earthenware. For his part, the first-century B.C. Roman poet Virgil recommended in the *Ecologues* that the hives should be weatherproofed against the winter and protected from the fierce summer sun by using mud smoothed over the outer surface.

Like the ancient Greeks, the Romans loved the taste of honey in their food and used it as a gift to their gods, so beekeeping flourished throughout the Roman empire. In the first century A.D., Apicius, a wealthy gourmet (though some called him a glutton) wrote a series of books in which more than half the recipes included honey. He used it not just in sweet dishes, but with ingredients such as meat, fish, vegetables, and nuts. Some of the recipes are exotic and inventive, to say the least: sweet melon with a savory sauce made from crushed pepper, herbs, and honey, followed by peacock marinaded in herbs and almonds and served with a honey, wine, and vinegar sauce. Whole hams were salted and smoked, boiled with figs and bay leaves, the skin scored and rubbed with honey, and the

These charming bees appears on a French sixteenth-century manuscript.

result finally baked whole in an oven, much as we might cook a ham today. Plainer foods were more commonly eaten, particularly a kind of cake-like bread known as *panis mellitus* (honey bread).

BEES IN THE WOODS

Central Europe had the perfect climate and environment for the production of honey. Thickly forested areas and a diversity of plant life meant good forage and cover for the bees. Poland and Germany, in particular, made great use of the products of the hive for food and drink. During a trip to the River Danube in the fifth century B.C., Herodotus, a much-traveled Greek historian, wrote that he found the river almost uncrossable at one point because of the concentration of bees gathered there. Once Christianity had become established, honey and beeswax production increased still further, partly to keep up with the enormous demand for church candles. This was to decrease suddenly, however, at the start of the Reformation many centuries later.

Taxes were often demanded in honey or beeswax. Charlemagne, king of the Franks from A.D. 771 to 814, instructed farmers to keep bees expressly for the purpose of paying tax, demanding two-thirds of their honey and one-third of their wax. French bureaucracy continued to be hard on the honey producers at various times through history, putting a tax both on beehives and on the common practice of honey hunting during the medieval period. In 1791, the French revolutionary government demanded a precise record of every hive in the country, resulting in a wholesale reduction in commercial beekeeping. And as late as 1934 a tax was yet again put on hives, supposedly to assess beekeeping along with the farming.

DRINKING HONEY

Long before the Roman invasion of Britain, the island was described by early Druid bards as "The Isle of Honey." Once the Romans arrived on the scene, Pliny commented that "these islanders consume copious quantities of the honeybrew." In fact, most of the population of central Europe drank brews of various kinds based on honey. Mead was an everyday drink when water was unsafe and tea and coffee were still unheard of. Russia had its own version of mead, plus a variant called *kvas*, made from barley or rye, salt, and a little honey. Mixed with

The dangers of disturbing the bees while extracting the honey can be seen in this thirteenth-century manuscript.

This nineteenth-century German print shows the process of straining honey into settling tanks to clear it. Although honey was less popular than sugar at this period, the tradition of beekeeping continued on a small scale.

24

The role of honey in medicine was achnowledged in **A Compleat History of Drugs** *by Pomet, published in London in 1725, as this plate from it shows.*

water and kept warm overnight, the mixture was stirred and left for a few more days until it was ready to drink. The result was refreshing and almost non-alcoholic, quite unlike mead.

Honey continued to be of vital importance to Europeans until the Renaissance, when the gradual influx of sugar from further afield

meant less and less honey was used. By the seventeenth century, sugar was well-established as a sweetener, and honey lost further ground. Once grain and hop-based ale became popular, the role of honey was minimal.

But in the New World, honey was gathering strength. The early settlers traveling to North America in the seventeenth century had taken hives of bees with them to provide valuable honey and beeswax. The insects adapted very well to the environment in Virginia and Massachusetts – the first areas to be colonized – and slowly spread west across the whole continent, reaching California by 1830. The country was already home to some indigenous types of bee, from which the native people took honey for cooking purposes.

Domestic bees were shipped to Australia in the 1800s, after a long and arduous journey following Captain Cook's route in the *Isabella*. These bees thrived on the Australian climate and rapidly multiplied, becoming the basis of a thriving modern honey industry. Today, North America and Australia dominate the world's production and export of honey.

Bee Emblems

Over the centuries, people of different cultures and religions have believed bees possess special attributes and powers and have taken the bee as their emblem. From the First Dynasty (3,200 B.C.), the bee was the sign of the king of Lower Egypt, and drawings and engravings of a single stylized bee are frequently found in tombs and on statues, wall paintings, and so on. The coffin of Men-Kau-ra (Fourth Dynasty, circa 2,500 B.C.) in the British Museum is one of the many early examples.

The Greeks called bees Birds of the Muse, because of their power to confer the gift of eloquence, and the Christian church believed bees to have strength and integrity because they swarmed away after the fall of man in the Garden of Eden. Mohammed viewed the bee with deference because, he claimed, the bee was the only animal who was addressed by the Lord himself.
Later historical figures who chose the bee as their emblem were Pope Urban VIII and Napoleon.

The emblem of Urban VIII, the 239th Pope, on the Basilica of St. Peter's in Rome.

Napoleon, resplendent in a robe decorated with his chosen emblem of single bees. His flag is cross-banded with a single line of bees in flight.

Health and Beauty

From the ancient Greek physicians to the followers of alternative medicine today, honey has always played an important role in the pursuit of health and beauty.

In the first century B.C. Hippocrates, the so-called father of modern medicine, praised honey's healing powers and regularly prescribed it to his patients. He formulated many honey-based cures for problems ranging from skin disorders, ulcers, and sores to sweating, respiratory complaints, and fevers.

26

Honey has always been enjoyed for its delicious taste, but it has also long been highly prized for its therapeutic and medicinal value. In the Old Testament Solomon advises "My son, eat thou honey" and the Koran proclaims that honey is "a medicine for men." Worldwide, it has been used in traditional forms of medicine and healing for as long as it has been taken from wild nests or domesticated hives. For less serious skin complaints, or simply to enhance beauty, honey has also been an important ingredient in cosmetics and beauty aids of all kinds.

Honey as a substance is quite complex. As a food, it contains 38 percent fructose, 31 percent glucose, 2 percent sucrose (all natural sugars), and 17 percent water. Natural honey will also contain small amounts of vitamins, such as thiamin, ascorbic acid, riboflavin, pantygiothenic acid, rydoxine, and niacin, but over-zealous filtering and heating can destroy these. Depending on the plants visited by the bees, the honey produced may also contain varying amounts of other substances, such as the mineral potassium, amino acids, and plant acids. It is thought that some specific flower honeys may have special properties because of substances in the nectar: eucalyptus honey, for example, may help in chest and respiratory complaints in the same way as eucalyptus oil from the tree.

One long-standing use of honey (recorded from as early as 2500 B.C. and still used today) is in the treatment of wounds and burns to the skin. The ancient Egyptians used honey in very many different medicines, but one particular document gives instructions for placing honey directly on the affected part of the body and wrapping it with a cloth as a dressing. This was used for open wounds, cuts, burns or ulcers, and if successful, the wound would dry out and heal satisfactorily with the minimum of scarring. The honey certainly forms a barrier to further infection from outside, and in fact, sugar has been used for a similar purpose.

On the Battlefield

It is believed that honey possesses the property of drawing out water from the cells of bacteria, causing them to dehydrate and die. It also contains an antibiotic substance called inhibine. As recently as World War I, German doctors were using honey mixed with cod liver oil to dress wounds surgically on the battlefront, and in some Eastern European countries the medical professions are still using it today.

It is difficult to substantiate much of the fact surrounding honey's healing properties, and there is still great scepticism about many of the fantastic claims made by honey's advocates. There is no doubt, however, that honey has stood the test of time. Much has been written

---

Sleep Enticer

The combination of chamomile, a natural sedative, and honey, believed to induce sleep, should result in a peaceful, uninterrupted slumber. The beverage is best sipped when tucked up in bed, propped up with a good book so that you can drift off to sleep.

1 chamomile tea bag
2tsp honey

Make a cup of chamomile tea with hot water and allow to cool until warm only. Stir in the honey and sip intermittently.

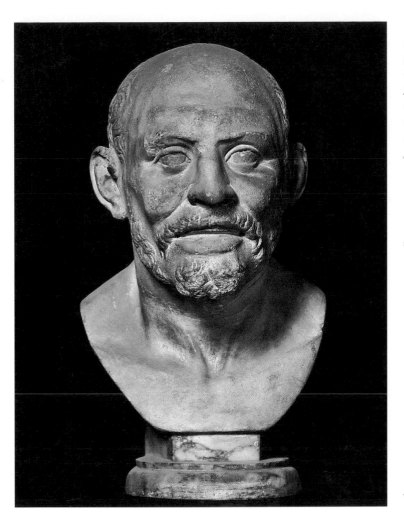

A near contemporary of Hippocrates, Democritus (the philosopher and physician), tried out many diets himself in the search for a formula for eternal life. He chose a diet with honey as an important part of it and supposedly lived until he was 109 years old.

Herbal Cold and Throat Syrup

To relieve all those irritating symptoms that accompany a cold, try this syrup. Sage is said to alleviate aches, pains, and fever.

$^1/_2$tsp chopped fresh or rubbed dried sage
3tbsp honey
2tbsp cider vinegar

Tie the sage in a gauze bag and steep in a cup half filled with boiling water for 10 minutes. Remove the sage and allow to cool.
Put the honey in a screwtop jar or bottle. Pour in the cider vinegar, then pour in the cooled sage water. Shake until well mixed.
Take 2 teaspoons every hour until the symptoms ease.

Propolis, or "beeglue," a by-product of honey, is gleaned from sticky plants and used in the hive to fill cracks and holes. Its antifungal and antiseptic properties make it a useful remedy for minor skin complaints.

27

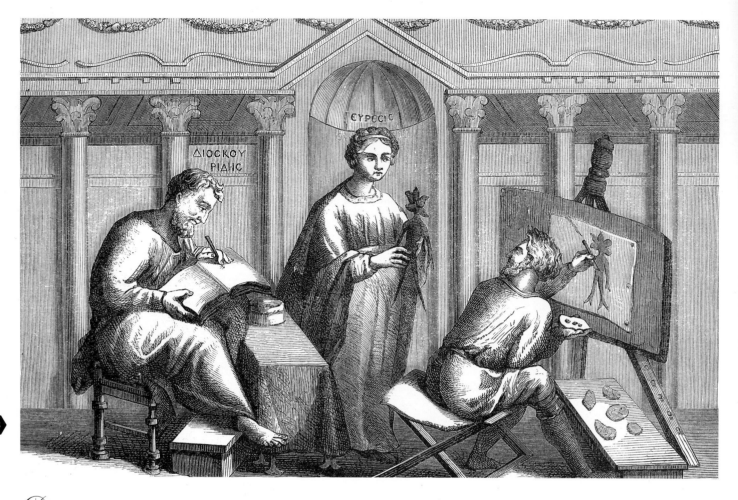

Dioscorides worked as a physician in Greece in the first century A.D. He claimed great powers for honey as a medicine, prescribing it for coughs, as a diuretic, for treating young and old alike, and even for cases of poisoning by toadstool, snake bite, or rabid dog.

Velvety Honey Conditioner

Based on an early eighteenth-century recipe secretly devised by England's Queen Anne, this enriching, creamy treatment will condition your hair and give it shine as well as leaving it velvety soft. Adding a couple of teaspoons of lemon juice will have a brightening effect on blond hair. The conditioner needs to be mixed just before it is needed, or it will separate before you are ready to use it.

2tbsp creamy set honey
1tbsp olive oil
¼tsp vanilla extract

Wash your hair as usual and towel it dry until just damp.
Place all the ingredients in a bowl and mix together using a hand beater; alternatively place the ingredients in a jar and shake vigorously. Smooth the conditioner liberally over the hair, combing it through with a wide-toothed comb to make sure it is evenly applied. Cover your head with a thin plastic shower cap. Warm your hair using a hairdrier for about five minutes; the heat causes the conditioner to penetrate the hair. Relax for 15 minutes, then remove the plastic cap and wash off the conditioner with a small amount of mild shampoo to remove excess oils.

over the centuries about its ability to heal wounds. A book of cures from the eighteenth century describes an episode where a woman in Rome suffered terrible burns over most of her body after her clothes caught alight. A servant hastily covered her burns with honey, and nine days later, according to the text, she was "perfectly cured by this remedy alone." An American doctor researching into the healing of wounds with honey wrote in 1973 that he had found "that honey when applied every two or three days under a dressing promotes the healing of wounds and ulcers better than any other local application I have ever used."

We are unlikely to find out how much truth, if any, there is in such claims until proper studies and research are carried out. As is the case with much "alternative" medicine, little research will be done while there are mass-produced, effective drugs available. However, as we move toward a time where many bacteria and diseases show signs of becoming immune to modern drugs, some practitioners believe natural healers will be taken more seriously.

One use for honey which most of us will probably have enjoyed and benefited from is as a soothing medicine for sore throats or irritating coughs. Honey had long been used as a sweet disguise for unpleasant-tasting medicines: being liquid, it mixed well with other ingredients and hid any bitterness or bad taste. There are delicious-sounding recipes for honey mixed with chopped sweet-scented rose or violet petals from medieval times. The rose version, known as "melrosette", was given as a medicine; although roses were essentially sweet and comforting, they were also seen as a cure for many kinds of ills. Most medieval honey mixtures had vile-tasting purging herbs, such as wormwood or rue, added to them so roses and violets were probably the attractive exception.

COUGHS AND COLDS

Dorothy Hartley, in her book *Food in England*, describes how country children who had ticklish coughs and sore throats were soothed by being given little balls of granulated honey creamed with butter. They would let the sweet rich mixture slowly dissolve in their mouths. Alison Uttley, the childrens' author, grew up in Derbyshire on a farm at the end of the last century and remembers morsels of butter,

Hangover Cure

After over-indulgence in alcohol, the second half of this recipe is useful for reducing unwanted hangover symptoms. However, if you know in advance that there is a possibility you might drink too much, take the first part of the cure before leaving home for the best results.

2¹/₂tbsp honey
½ cup milk
1 lemon, juice only

Mix 1 tablespoon of the honey with the milk, and drink this before any anticipated over-indulgence of alcohol to line the stomach.
On returning home, mix the remainder of the honey with the lemon juice and ½ cup water to accelerate the liver's processing rate.

honey, and lemon being prescribed for a cold. She describes a cough medicine made from salad oil, paregoric (a camphor mixture), lemon juice, and honey. Today, all manner of commercial cough soothers are still based around honey and are generally combined with lemon juice to provide a dose of vitamin C. The traditional hot lemon, honey, and whiskey cold

A tincture of propolis is used as a natural infection fighter against such problems as sore throats, the common cold, and mouth and gum disorders. At one time violin makers used propolis in their wood varnish.

29

Lemon and Honey Throat Soother

An old favorite, this concoction is effective for treating mild sore throats. It can be used as a gargle to soothe the throat, and can then be swallowed to gain maximum benefit from the ingredients. If you omit the ginger, the mixture makes a good cough mixture, to be taken one teaspoon at a time as needed.

3tbsp honey
1 lemon, juice only
2tsp vegetable glycerin
¹/₄tsp ground ginger

Place the honey and lemon in a small bowl and stir until well mixed. Add the vegetable glycerin, stirring until smooth. Stir in the ginger. Gargle and swallow 1 teaspoon every hour.

Poppea, the beloved wife of the Emperor Nero, instructed her servants to put a mixture of honey and asses' milk on her face regularly to keep the skin smooth and youthful.

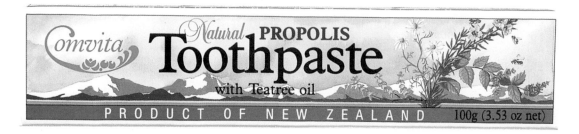

Propolis has been claimed to have all kinds of beneficial properties. Here it has found its way into a natural toothpaste.

A fine skin was considered essential by the Egyptians. This relief from Denderah shows Cleopatra exposing more than a little of hers, but it would have been softened and smoothed by baths of honey and asses' milk.

cure is as popular as ever, with good reason, but try the Herbal Cold and Throat Remedy or the Lemon and Honey Throat Soother if you prefer a different, non-alcoholic version. If all the ingredients are not on hand when you develop a sudden cough or sore throat, try taking a spoonful of liquid honey and swallow it slowly, letting it get to work on the painful throat.

These all seem to be rather delicious medicines, but an old traditional English remedy for earache is certainly one to avoid. A small piece of peeled onion was dipped in honey and inserted into the ear – how long it was left there is uncertain! There may have been some common sense in this, though, as onion is a known antiseptic. However, the risk of further infection outweighs the potential benefits from this rather unappealing cure.

There have long been claims that honey can be beneficial to sufferers of chest complaints such as asthma and bronchitis. Tests carried out at the Medical Research Department in Lansing, Michigan, after World War II found that hay-fever sufferers appeared to benefit from a diet which included honey, especially if small amounts of pollen were still in the unrefined honey. The researchers also noticed that chewing the honey-filled comb had an even more beneficial effect. Some alternative health practitioners suggest a course of pollen-rich local honey before the hay fever season begins, as a way of boosting resistance to the affecting pollen.

Beeswax, too, has long been used as a primitive kind of chewing gum. There are medieval recipes for it combining wax, honey, ginger, and cinnamon with oil of terebinth, which came from fir trees and gave the gum a resinous pine flavor.

AND SO TO BED

Honey reputedly also has a soporific effect, so has often been used to make sleep-inducing potions. Gypsy recipes, for example, use the juice of lemons and oranges mixed with honey and diluted with hot water, to be drunk before retiring for the night. That well-known sleep promoter, warm milk, is supposed to have an even faster effect if sweetened with a spoonful of honey, but it is not really surprising that such a concoction might induce sleep. Milk and honey is the stuff of myth and legend, and on a more basic level, a mug of it is likely to remind us of carefree childhood bedtimes or even

Cleansing Morning Tonic

There is no better way to start the day than with this refreshing tonic. The benefits are several: it cleans out the system; it is a mild laxative; it promotes a healthy, well-functioning liver; and it is good for skin blemishes. For maximum benefit, take this tonic every morning before breakfast.

3tsp honey
½ lemon, juice only

Mix the honey and lemon juice with ½ cup of lukewarm water, and drink.

Rich Honey Hand Balm

Ideal for soothing dry hands, this moisturizing, satiny, rose-scented balm uses beeswax to protect skin from adverse conditions, and olive oil to give extra smoothness. It is also good for restoring moisture to tired hands, rough elbows, or chapped lips. Beeswax granules are available from health-food stores.

1tsp beeswax granules
½tsp olive oil
1tbsp honey
1–2 drops rose essential oil

Place the beeswax granules and olive oil in a small bowl set over a saucepan of simmering water. Allow the wax to melt; then turn off the heat. With the bowl still set over the saucepan, quickly stir in the honey and rose oil. Stir until smooth, then pour into a small jar and allow to set. When it is just warm, stir with your finger or the handle of a spoon until creamy.
To use, first place your hands or elbows in warm water and dry them; the balm is easier to apply to warmed skin. Place a dab of balm in your palm and massage in to the skin until your hands feel smooth and soft.
Remove excess balm with a tissue.
For your lips, simply apply with your fingertips or a lip brush.

sleepy babyhood hours at the breast or bottle. The physicians of ancient Rome used honey to help their patients get to sleep and were so impressed by its potency that they felt obliged to warn patients of its potential strength, lest they did not wake up at daybreak. Of course, this might just have been a clever way of absolving themselves from any blame should their patients die in their sleep due to the physician's negligence.

The Romans believed that honey had a tonic effect on the whole gastrointestinal area and prescribed it as a gentle but efficient laxative – and oddly, as a cure for diarrhea, too. Research has been carried out on the use of honey as a treatment for diarrhea, with claims that common gut bacteria such as salmonella, chigella, and *E. coli* cannot survive in honey. (This may be the same principle as preserving foods with sugar so that the bacteria cannot survive in the concentrated sweet environment.)

THE ENERGY GIVER
By the seventeenth century in Britain, ideas about the beneficial medicinal uses of honey were quite wide-ranging. Often based on writings of the Greeks and other ancients, few facts could be scientifically proven, but would come from observation, experience, and the research of others. In 1623, a keen British beekeeper called Charles Butler wrote a book called *History of Bees*. Based on the writings of a first century Greek physician known as Dioscorides, Butler claimed that "Honey clears up all the instructions of the body, loosens the belly, purges the foulness of the body, provokes urine, cuts down phlegm, restores the appetite, takes away that which damages the eyes and nourishes very much." He went on to say that it bred good blood, preserved natural heat and prolonged life.

Marguerite de Navarre, wife of King Henri IV of France, was one of many French beauties who swore by the regular use of honey to maintain her beautiful complexion.

Agnes Sorel, the mistress of Charles VII of France, was known as la Dame de Beaute from the name of the estate the besotted King gave her. She was a passionate advocate of honey both as a cosmetic and in the form of a spice cake invented in honor of Charles at Dijon containing strong buckwheat honey from Brittany.

Commercial versions of honey water for the hair were obviously available early this century. This one is described as a wash and a pomade. A pomade was more likely to be used by a man, as a dressing or treatment for the hair.

EXTRACT OF
Honey and Flowers

Combines both the qualities of a Wash and Pomade; it gently stimulates the growth of the Hair, and imparts to it a soft and brilliant appearance.

Shake the Bottle before application.

.. PREPARED BY ..
F. M. PFOB,
2 Royal Arcade, Norwich.

Interestingly, all these claims for honey seem to have been popular at one time or another in various countries and cultures. That honey is nourishing is well known, and athletes, from runners in the original Olympic Games in ancient Greece to modern-day climbers and English Channel swimmers, have taken advantage of its speedy energy-boosting qualities. Because honey is made up of fructose and glucose, it has a two-tier energy supply. The glucose is quickly absorbed by the body and gives an immediate boost, while the fructose works more slowly to provide a sustained amount of energy. Experiments on athletes earlier this century in Toronto showed that those who took honey before and after competing recovered more quickly from their exertions than those who relied on other forms of sugar. Being an alkaline food, honey is broken down by saliva more quickly during the first stage of digestion within the mouth. Additionally, both glucose and fructose are

Geranium Softening Facial

The geranium oil in this penetrating facial mask improves the blood circulation around the face, giving it a healthy glow. The mask softens and hydrates the skin, leaving it smooth and silky.

2tbsp whipping cream
1 egg, yolk only
1tbsp creamy set honey
1–2 drops geranium essential oil

In a bowl, whip the cream until it is beginning to thicken and soft peaks are just forming. Beat in the egg yolk until fluffy, then add the honey and geranium essential oil, beating until evenly blended.
Using a large cosmetic or blusher brush, apply the mixture to your face and neck. Relax for 20 minutes while the mask does its work. Rinse the mask off with warm water and splash your face and neck with cold water or toner to tighten the pores.

Fragrant Lemon Deep-Cleansing Treatment

Fresh and deep-cleansing, this treatment opens skin pores and refines the complexion. It is ideal as a preparation before applying a deep-cleansing mask treatment.

1tbsp clear honey
2–3 drops lemon essential oil

Using a large cosmetic brush or wet fingertips, apply the honey thinly to your face and relax for 10 minutes to allow the honey time to soften the skin. When ready, pour boiling water into a bowl and add the lemon essential oil. Lean over the bowl and place a towel over your head and the bowl so that the steam can work on your pores. When the steam stops rising, rinse off any honey left on the skin. Finally, splash your face with cold water to close the pores.

said to be highly digestible. It appears that bees have already done some of the work for our alimentary system by partially digesting the sugars themselves, so the honey is quickly and easily absorbed by our bodies without any irritation to our digestive system. That honey "prolongs life" is another claim that has been widely held over the centuries with a few cases of people reaching an amazing age and citing honey as the cause of their longevity. The ancient Greek physician Hippocrates was convinced of honey's ability to prolong life and his near contemporary, the philosopher and physicist Democritus, supposedly managed to live for 109 years, thanks to following a diet based on honey.

BATHING IN BEAUTY

Honey may or may not be a dietary formula for eternal youth, but when added to cosmetics, it has long been used to delay or counteract the effects of aging on the skin. It would appear that its healing properties, harnessed so dramatically for the treatment of wounds, can also help in day-to-day skin care for face, hands, and body. There are many references over the centuries to the use of honey as a cosmetic, particularly by the rich and powerful women of their time. Whether it was also more commonly used by the mass of people, it is harder to discover, though presumably ordinary people with access to honey might have accidentally discovered how soft and smooth their hands became after contact with it.

Cleopatra is remembered for her famous baths of asses' milk, which supposedly contained honey. Bath is probably the wrong word for this beauty treatment, since a further washing must have been needed to remove the

It is claimed that Queen Anne used a honey and oil concoction to keep her long hair lustrous, thick, and shiny. In this portrait she has her hair long and natural in the romantic style of the early 1700s.

33

sweet stickiness from her skin. Poppea, the wife of the Roman emperor Nero, also used the honey skin treatment, and regularly instructed her servants to smear a honey and milk lotion over her face to keep her looking youthful. Chinese women have a tradition of using a blend of honey and ground orange seeds to keep their skins blemish-free, and in Japan honey was used as a softening hand lotion. The French have always been dedicated to the pursuit of beauty, and many famous French women from every century seem to have used honey as part of their toilette. Agnes Sorel, the

Madame du Barry is served her morning chocolate and looks elegant and perfectly coiffed already. Writings of the period tell us that her skin benefited from frequent applications of honey.

Oatmeal Exfoliating Mask

The combination of honey and oatmeal makes the perfect treatment for a dull or oily skin. The mask is gently removed after the treatment, lifting off dead skin cells and leaving the complexion clear and fresh.

1 egg, yolk only
2tbsp clear honey
3tbsp finely ground oatmeal
1tsp orange water

In a bowl, beat together the egg yolk and honey until velvety. Sprinkle in the oatmeal and blend well. Finally, add the orange water to scent the mixture.
Using a large cosmetic brush, paint the oatmeal over your face and neck to cover them completely, avoiding the eyes.
Relax with a good book or lie down for 20 minutes.
When the treatment has taken effect, gently rub your face and neck with your fingertips to loosen the oatmeal mask.
Remove the mask with a washcloth or cotton pads moistened with warm water.

mistress of Charles VII, used it in the fifteenth century and called it "the soul of flowers." Coincidentally, she also had a passion for honey in a different form – in spiced bread, of which she claimed she would never tire. Madame du Barry, the infamous last mistress of Louis XV, used honey as a form of facial mask, lying down for a rest while the honey did its work. Later, the honey was rinsed away with warm water – an idea we could copy, but one which is probably best done while in the bath. Try the Geranium Softening Facial (page 32) when your face needs pampering.

Honey and Buttermilk Cleanser

Made from honey and buttermilk with a dash of rosewater, this cleanser is inspired by the famous beauty treatment used by Cleopatra and many other beautiful women in history. It will leave the skin feeling refreshed, silky soft, and clean.

2tsp clear honey
1tbsp buttermilk
1/4tsp rosewater

Beat all the ingredients together in a bowl and apply the cleanser to your face, neck, and shoulders using your fingertips. Splash off with lukewarm water, then pat the skin dry.

Most research into the uses of honey as a beauty preparation suggest that it was used mainly for skin treatments, but there are records of it being made into hair lotions and tonics, too. In England Queen Anne, who was said to have taken enormous pride in her appearance, invented a preparation to keep her hair healthy and lustrous. As none of her ladies-in-waiting dared to risk asking her for the secret, it was not revealed until her death in 1714. Her hair conditioner consisted of honey beaten with olive oil of, no doubt, the finest quality. It reputedly gave her hair a marvelous shine and has been used by women in some form or other ever

Lavender Tightening Facial Mask

Wonderfully fragrant, this mask will tighten skin, leaving it silky but taut. It is a good, quick facial pick-me-up before an important night out.

1tbsp clear honey
2tsp thick yogurt
1 egg, white only
2–3 drops lavender essence

In a bowl, beat the honey and yogurt together until smooth and well blended. Add the egg white and lavender essence, mixing until silky smooth.
Using a cosmetic brush or your fingertips, smooth the mask over your face, taking care to avoid the eye and lip areas. Leave the mask in place for 10–15 minutes; you will feel the tightening effect on your skin as it dries.
Rinse the mask off with lukewarm water, and splash your face with your favorite toner or flower water.

Honey water has been popular as a face freshener or tonic for centuries.

since. Try the recipe for Velvety Honey Conditioner (page 28) for yourself. Another English beauty, Sarah, Duchess of Marlborough, was also credited with having beautiful hair. Judging by portrait paintings of the time, a woman's hair was expected to be long, natural-looking, and romantically swept into gentle curls. (This was before the era of outrageous powdered artificial wigs.) A contemporary of the Duchess once wrote of her that "she had the most beautiful head of hair imaginable, the colour of which she had preserved unchanged by the constant use of honey water." Sarah and Anne had been firm friends until they quarreled in later life. So perhaps they shared the secret of using honey to keep their hair in beautiful condition.

By the time cosmetics were beginning to be mass-produced at the end of the nineteenth century, honey was a popular ingredient. Then, as now, its connotations of naturalness, the outdoors, and good health made it attractive. Beeswax has also always been used as an emulsifying agent and an important ingredient of creams and lotions as it is a pure and easily obtainable, though expensive, product. It is included in the recipe for rich Honey Hand Balm. The simplest uses of honey are often the best. For example, a mixture of ground almonds, oatmeal, honey, and egg yolk makes a marvelous cleanser and softener for hard-worked hands that have been gardening or doing too much housework. Or try a similar recipe for Oatmeal Exfoliating Mask, this time for the face.

An engraving of one of many portraits made of Sarah, Duchess of Marlborough who was famed for the beauty of her hair. It was claimed that she used her own secret recipe for a honey water to keep it in such good condition.

A World of Honey

Many stores and supermarkets now stock a wide selection of honeys, and the displays in specialist outlets can be bewildering, especially for the novice. Honeys vary in color from almost white to nearly black; they may be clear or opaque and, while some of their names are comfortingly recognizable, some are exotic and strange. Fortunately, things are not as complicated as they might appear at first glance.

Clear honey is fairly fluid and is in virtually the same state as it was in the hive. It has only been strained through a cloth or fine mesh to remove any debris. Occasionally it is heat-treated to prevent crystallization. It is usually a lovely pale or golden amber color, but can be darker, even almost black, depending on the flowers from which it was made.

Creamy set honey is thick and opaque. It is granulated honey from which some of the moisture has been removed. The color of this type of honey ranges from almost white to creamy, to dark yellow. Creamy set honeys are easy to spread – just right for hot toast.

All honeys are sweet, but when it comes to tasting them individually, it is surprising how much variety there is. The range of scents and flavors is also astonishing, and depends on the type of flowers used by the bees. Some flavors are distinctive, others only just subtly different from the next.

A honey is termed multi-flower if the bees were allowed to pick and choose the nectar from a range of vegetation, making up their own unique recipe. Single-flower honey may sound simpler, but it requires more skill on the part of the beekeeper to make sure that the bees take the nectar largely from one specific type of flower; there will always be a stray blossom or two along the route the bee travels. One way to do this is to transport the hives physically to the place where a particular flower or crop is in bloom and leave them there until the flowering is over. The honey has to be harvested before the hive is moved on to another spot, perhaps as a different crop comes into flower. The other way to ensure single-flower honey is for the beekeeper to be so totally in tune with the seasons as to know just when a particular type of plant is in flower and, therefore, possibly dominant. As soon as the flowering of that particular plant is over, to the day, the beekeeper must remove the honey.

Blended honey is made up of several varieties. Blending honey is a little like blending wine and is a way of creating a uniform honey from undistinguished harvests, with a sustainable texture and flavor that will appeal to a wide audience. To do this requires some skill in identifying bouquet, assessing color and savoring flavor. A professional honey taster or blender can "nose" a honey to identify the flower and assess the flavor.

Cut comb honey is just what it says: a piece of the comb with honey still in the cells cut and packed into a jar with pale liquid honey poured around it. You get the wax, honey, pollen – and any other bits and pieces!

Selection honey is sold as a complete square or block of comb contained in a small wooden frame packaged into a box or wrapped securely in cellophane. This is difficult to produce commercially and nowadays is quite a rarity. Consequently, it has become a luxury.

The honeybee has a fantastic array of flowers at its disposal. In theory, anything that contains nectar is worth investigating, but which blossoms a bee or group of bees decides to home in on will depend upon local availability at a given time of year and preference.

These bees have been irresistibly attracted to this jar of honey, even though the honey itself has been processed and is no longer in the pure state they are used to in the hive.

As this sampling shows, honeys can be either clear or creamy, though a few partly granulated or crystallized varieties achieve a middle path between the two. Lighter-colored honeys tend to be milder in flavor.

ACACIA HONEY

A clear honey produced in eastern Europe and many other parts of the world. It is a pale, light color with a hint of gold, and has a thin and runny consistency. Its flavor, of heavily scented flowers, is sweeter than that of most honeys.

CHESTNUT HONEY

A clear honey from the French Pyrenees and northern Italy. The color is a lovely dark reddish-gold, and it has quite a thick consistency. The rich, nutty flavor of burnt roasted chestnuts has a slightly bitter, tannin-like undertone.

BUCKWHEAT HONEY

A clear honey made from the buckwheat crops of the USA and China. Extremely dark, almost black in color, it has a thick consistency. The intense flavor is somewhat like molasses, and it has a pungent, earthy aroma. It is often used in blends.

GREEK MOUNTAIN HONEY

A clear honey gathered in Greek mountains. It is a dark toffee-brown with a medium to thick consistency. Its wonderfully strong taste is of pine and herbs with a slightly medicinal undertone, and its scent captures the rich bouquet of Mediterranean flowers and herbs.

LEATHERWOOD HONEY

A clear set honey unique to the west coast of Tasmania in Australia. Golden amber in color, it has a medium to thin consistency. The flavor is reminiscent of the heady scent of flowers on a hot summer's day, and it has a highly perfumed aroma.

HEATHER HONEY

Not quite clear and sometimes rather dense, this honey is gathered from the moorlands and open woodlands of northern and western Europe. Golden amber with red overtones, its slightly gelatinous texture makes it almost chewy. The flavor is mildly sweet, a little bitter and grassy, with a pleasing aftertaste of burnt caramel.

CLOVER HONEY

A usually clear, but sometimes creamy, set honey, produced from ground flora grown as animal fodder in Britain, Canada, the USA, Australia, and New Zealand. It is light amber and has a fairly thin consistency. It is very sweet with a delicate, freshly mown lawn scent.

LIME BLOSSOM HONEY

A clear honey, usually from eastern Europe or the USA. It is a light amber color with a greenish tinge and has a thin, runny consistency. Made from the blossom of the lime or linden tree, it has no connection with the citrus fruit lime. It has a strong, heady aroma and tang.

EUCALYPTUS HONEY

A clear honey produced in Australia. It is quite dark in color with a medium to thin consistency. Its distinctive taste, not as strong as the color would suggest, is of dried raisins mixed with the fresh, stringent scents of the Australian bush.

LAVENDER HONEY

A clear honey, usually from areas bordering the Mediterranean, notably the Provence region of France. It is a pale golden color with a medium consistency. The delicate flavor is reminiscent of lavender flowers and quite sweet, though it ends with a touch of tartness.

MANUKA HONEY

A clear honey from the New Zealand manuka tree. It is a dense caramel brown with a fairly thick and sticky consistency, similar to that of heather honey. The unique flavor is medicinal, slightly bitter, and tannin-like with caramel overtones.

STRAWBERRY CLOVER HONEY

A creamy set honey taken from the strawberry clover flower in South Australia. The color is an unusual muddy, creamy white. Being very thick, it is a little difficult to handle, but the sweet, buttery taste, reminiscent of caramels, makes any effort worthwhile.

OILSEED RAPE HONEY

A creamy set honey from the oilseed rape crop found throughout Europe. The color is a yellow-tinged white, and the consistency is very thin and runny. Very sweet and creamy tasting with a slightly oily aftertaste, it is often used in blends.

THYME HONEY

A clear honey from wild plants in the Provence region of France and the Greek mountains. It is a rich dark amber in color with a medium consistency. The strong herb flavor has a slightly bitter aftertaste.

CANADIAN CLOVER HONEY

A creamy set honey from Canada. It is rich, luscious creamy white with a velvety texture. Its medium consistency is just right for spreading. The flavor is reminiscent of vanilla, combined with the scent of beeswax candles.

SUNFLOWER HONEY

A creamy set honey from Europe. It has a rich, creamy yellow color and a very thick consistency, second only to that of strawberry clover. The flavor is mildly sweet, distinctly oily and waxy, and reminiscent of the countryside.

39

ORANGE BLOSSOM HONEY

A superbly fragrant clear honey from Israel, Malta, Spain, the USA, and Mexico. Light amber in color and thin to medium in consistency, it is fairly sweet with a flavor full of almonds and orange rind.

ROSEMARY HONEY

A clear herb honey from the Mediterranean. It has a lovely dense but light golden color and a thick, slightly gelatinous consistency similar to that of heather honey, with a tendency to crystallize. The taste is sweet and floral with a hint of the herb.

TUPELO HONEY

A clear honey unique to Florida. It is pale gold in color and has a very thin and runny consistency. The delicate but fragrant taste is of spring flowers and is fairly sweet.

CHAPTER ONE

FIRST COURSES

Honey is a perfect ingredient in quick snacks and first courses, providing both an instant boost of energy and unusual flavors. From French toast dusted with cinnamon to prosciutto and eggplant crostini, honey can be the ingredient that transforms the conventional into the sublime.

FIRST COURSES

With the pace of modern life, a relaxed, formal meal is becoming more and more of a luxury. The appetizer sets the tone for the whole meal, so why restrict it to assorted salad leaves and croutons or limp shrimp cocktails? Just add a touch of delicately flavored honey to transform a simple vinaigrette. Or add orange juice and honey to create a bittersweet infusion to complement a classic chicory and orange salad.

For a suppertime treat, indulge yourself with hot toasted muffins or bagels spread with honey. Turn a simple yogurt into a delicious and nutritious snack with a spoonful of honey and some chopped nuts, or fresh fruit – strawberries are ideal – chopped roughly and bathed in clear honey. For something a little more sophisticated, light pancakes smothered in honey and lemon juice are simply delicious.

Holyday, *James Tissot, 1876*

SMOKED TROUT *with* MUSTARD *and* TARRAGON SAUCE

Delicately flavored acacia honey adds a certain sweetness and softness to the dressing in this dish. To achieve the best results, make the dressing an hour or so in advance and place it in a refrigerator to allow time for the tarragon to diffuse its flavor.

SERVES 4

2tbsp Dijon mustard	*4tbsp light cream*
1tbsp acacia honey	*4 smoked trout fillets*
3tsp tarragon-flavored white wine vinegar	*¼ lb oak leaf lettuce, or similar leaves*
1tsp finely chopped fresh tarragon	*salad cress, snipped freshly ground black pepper*

To make the sauce, combine the mustard, honey, and white wine vinegar in a small bowl. Mix until smooth, then add the tarragon and stir in the cream.

Arrange the lettuce leaves on individual plates. Break up each trout fillet and distribute the flesh evenly over the lettuce leaves. Drizzle the mustard and tarragon dressing over, then sprinkle with the snipped cress.

Season with freshly ground black pepper and serve.

Bears like Honey

In literature, bears and a love of honey are almost synonymous, the most famous fictional one of honey fans being A.A. Milne's Winnie the Pooh. In real life, bears like the Himalayan black bear and the Indian sloth bear will go to great lengths to indulge their taste, showing enormous ingenuity to reach even the remotest hives.

COMPOTE *of* ORANGE, FIG, *and* DATE *with a* CRUNCHY GRANOLA

46

The raisin-like flavor of eucalyptus honey marries well with the fresh and dried fruits of this compote. Excellent as a breakfast dish, it can double as a dessert if you replace the pine-nut granola with a portion of crème fraîche or Greek-style yogurt. Dried figs can be used in place of fresh ones but will require longer cooking; add them to the syrup with the orange segments and dates.

SERVES 4

5oz eucalyptus honey	*16 dried dates*
4tbsp orange-flavored liqueur	*4 fresh figs, halved*
2in cinnamon stick	GRANOLA
4 cloves	*½ cup porridge oats*
2 oranges, peeled, segmented,	*1tbsp pine nuts*
and with pith removed	*1tbsp sunflower seeds*

Place the honey, orange-flavored liqueur, cinnamon stick, and cloves in a saucepan with ½ cup of water. Bring to a boil, then simmer for 5-8 minutes until the liquid starts to thicken and become syrupy.

Add the orange segments and dates and simmer for 15 minutes. Add the figs and simmer for a further 5 minutes. Allow the compote to cool, then chill in the refrigerator for at least 2 hours before serving.

To make the granola, heat a skillet until hot, then add the oats, pine nuts, and sunflower seeds. Turn the heat down to medium and toast for about 1 minute until golden brown. Serve sprinkled over the compote.

CHILLED MINT *and* HONEY SOUP *with* POPPADOMS

Sweet and savory flavors are successfully mixed in this chilled mint soup, which makes a refreshing summer dish and an interesting prelude to an Indian meal.

SERVES 4

¼ cup salted butter	*4tbsp whole mint leaves*
4 shallots, roughly chopped	*pinch salt*
1 honeydew or any white-	*½ cup light cream*
fleshed melon, seeded and	*4tbsp Greek-style yogurt*
chopped	*4 plain poppadoms, ready for*
1¾ cups vegetable stock	*cooking*
1tbsp clear honey	*1tbsp roughly chopped mint*
1¼tbsp white wine vinegar	*leaves for garnish*

Melt the butter in a saucepan, add the shallots, and sauté for 2-3 minutes until soft. Add the melon and cook for 2-3 minutes. Pour in the vegetable stock and simmer for about 5 minutes. Allow to cool.

Pour the contents of the saucepan into a food processor, add the honey, white wine vinegar, and the whole mint leaves and blend until smooth. Add salt to taste.

Pour the mixture into a bowl, add the cream and 2 tablespoons of the yogurt, then whip briefly. Chill in the freezer for 40-60 minutes before serving.

While the soup is chilling, cook the poppadoms. Place one at a time in a microwave oven on high for 30 seconds, or until it puffs up. Alternatively cook under a medium-hot grill for 1-2 minutes, turning halfway through cooking.

Remove the soup from the freezer and whip lightly if settled. Serve in individual bowls topped with ½ tablespoon yogurt and a sprinkling of chopped mint.

Dreaming of Honey

"Hide me from day's garish eye,
While the bee, with honeyed thigh,
That at her flowering work doth sing,
And the waters murmuring,
with such consort as they keep,
Entice the dewy-feather'd sleep."

IL PENSEROSO, JOHN MILTON

LEEK TERRINE *with* HONEY *and* MUSTARD VINAIGRETTE

Pink peppercorns delicately flavor this light, creamy terrine, while honey adds sweetness to the vinaigrette, countering the acidity and making a smooth sauce. Served warm, it will keep out the cold on cool days; chilled, it is perfect for a hot summer's day.

SERVES 4

2lb leeks	*2 eggs*
¼ cup butter	*hot pepper sauce to taste*
3tbsp roughly chopped chives	VINAIGRETTE
plus whole chives for	*1tbsp Dijon mustard*
garnish	*1tbsp clear honey*
3tbsp white wine	*1tsp pink peppercorns*
1tsp pink peppercorns	*2tbsp white wine vinegar*
6tbsp light cream	*6tbsp olive oil*
1tsp Dijon mustard	*freshly ground black pepper*

Heat the oven to 350°F.

Trim 4 of the leeks to fit lengthwise in a 4 cup loaf pan. Bring a saucepan of water to a boil and cook the trimmed leeks for 2-3 minutes until they start turning bright green and are slightly softened. Remove them from the pan and plunge them in cold water to stop the cooking process. Pat them dry with paper towels and set aside.

Slice the remaining leeks into rounds. Melt the butter in a skillet, add the sliced leeks, and cook for 4-5 minutes until tender and soft. Allow to cool slightly, then place in a food processor with the chopped chives, the white wine, peppercorns, cream, mustard, eggs, and a couple of shakes of hot pepper sauce to taste. Process for 30-40 seconds until the leeks are roughly chopped.

Place a spoonful of the chopped leek mixture in the bottom of the greased loaf pan, arrange the four whole leeks on top and pour over the balance of the mixture. Cover the pan with foil and place it in a *bain-marie*, or a deep baking pan with enough boiling water to reach halfway up the sides of the pan. Place in the oven and bake for 45-50 minutes until set.

To make the vinaigrette, place all the ingredients in a jar with a screw-on lid and shake vigorously until mixed.

Remove the terrine from the oven and allow to cool. Unmold it by running a knife around the edges, then cut into slices using a very sharp knife. Serve warm or cold, garnished with whole chives and accompanied by the vinaigrette.

HONEYED RICOTTA *with* FRUIT CRUDITÉS

Ricotta cheese is an excellent vehicle for the heady, almost almondy sweetness of orange blossom honey. Served with exotic, or any kind of fresh fruit, it makes a healthy, nutritious snack or an adventurous appetizer. It is also good spread on crackers.

SERVES 4

1lb ricotta cheese	*1 honeydew melon*
3tbsp orange blossom honey	*1 mango*
1 papaya	

Mix the ricotta cheese and honey in a large bowl until well blended. Spoon the mixture into four small heart-shaped perforated molds lined with paper towel. Press the ricotta down gently, then place on a tray to catch moisture from the ricotta. Chill in the refrigerator for 1-2 hours.

Meanwhile, cut the skin off the papaya, melon and mango. Slice into thin strips lengthwise.

To unmold, take the paper towel and lift the cheese out of the molds. Turn out the shaped ricottas onto individual plates and surround each with strips of fruit.

WHOLE-WHEAT PANCAKES *with* HONEY *and* CRISP BACON

Topped with whipped butter and piping hot crispy bacon, this scrumptious snack is made with honey reflecting the North American love of mixing sweet and tart. It is perfect for brunch or a light meal.

SERVES 4

1¼ cups stoneground whole- wheat flour	TOPPING
pinch salt	6 tbsp salted butter, at room temperature
1¼ cups whole milk	1tsp light cream
1 egg	8 slices bacon
2tsp acacia honey, warmed	1tbsp acacia honey

Put the flour into a large bowl and make a well in the center with a spoon. Sprinkle in a good pinch of salt.

Pour the milk into another bowl, add the egg and beat together until well mixed. Drizzle the warmed honey into the egg mixture, beating constantly.

Pour half of the egg mixture into the well in the flour and, using a fork, whip the liquid gently without touching the flour; this allows small amounts of flour to slip into the liquid from the sides without forming any lumps. Continue whipping until the pancake batter is smooth.

Add the rest of the egg mixture, whipping quickly with the fork. Set the batter aside until needed.

For the topping, place the butter and the cream in a bowl and beat with an electric beater or by hand until creamy and light. Leave at room temperature until needed.

Place a skillet over a medium to high heat, add the bacon, and fry for 8-10 minutes until the bacon is crisp and all the milky liquid has evaporated.

Meanwhile, heat a small nonstick skillet until hot. If you do not have one, use an ordinary skillet with some butter. Cook the pancakes one at a time using about ¼ cup of the batter for each pancake. Cook on one side for about 1 minute, and when the batter begins to form small bubbles, turn the pancake using a pancake turner. Cook the other side for 1 minute until browned. Place each cooked pancake on a warmed serving plate.

To serve, drizzle 1 teaspoon of honey over each pancake, add a dollop of whipped butter and 2 slices of crisp bacon.

CINNAMON *and* HONEY FRENCH TOAST

French toast is a clever way of transforming stale bread into something delectable. The addition of honey makes it even more delicious – perfect for a leisurely brunch or a self-indulgent snack at any time of the day.

SERVES 4

8 slices stale white bread	1¼ cups whole milk
4tbsp clear honey	¼ cup salted butter
2 eggs	2tsp ground cinnamon

Spread one side of each slice of bread with 1 teaspoon of honey and leave it for a few minutes to soak into the bread. In a large flat casserole dish, beat the eggs with 1½ tablespoons of the honey with a fork until blended. Add the milk, beating for another minute or so.

Melt the butter and 2 teaspoons of honey in a large flat-based skillet; keep it over a very low heat until the bread is ready to be cooked.

Dip one slice of bread at a time in the egg mixture, allowing it to absorb the liquid for 8-10 seconds; do not let it get too soggy or it will fall apart.

Turn the skillet heat up to high. When the skillet is hot, put in 2 slices of bread and cook for 2-3 minutes on each side until golden brown; cooking only 2 slices at a time prevents the bread from sticking together in an overcrowded pan.

Sprinkle each slice with ¼ teaspoon of cinnamon and serve warm.

Sweetness & Light

"Instead of dirt and poison we have rather chosen to fill our hives with honey and wax; thus furnishing mankind with the two noblest things, which are sweetness and light."

JONATHAN SWIFT, 1667–1745

This ceramic box has been designed to resemble a honeycomb – the bees make delightful motifs.

52

PROSCIUTTO *and* EGGPLANT CROSTINI

The topping for these crostini (Italian toasted bread) is inspired by the ancient Roman practice of glazing ham with honey. Prosciutto is an intensely flavored Italian cured ham, and the use of rosemary honey reinforces the Mediterranean origin of the dish. Ciabatta, a flattish Italian bread, is available from many supermarkets and bakeries, but other white breads could be substituted.

MAKES 12

1 eggplant
¾ cup olive oil
4tbsp roughly chopped fresh oregano plus torn leaves for garnish

2 large cloves garlic, crushed
1 ciabatta loaf
2tsp rosemary honey
12 slices of bacon

Heat the oven to 425°F.

Slice the eggplant into 24 ½-inch thick circles and place them on a baking sheet. Brush them liberally with olive oil on both sides. Sprinkle half of the chopped oregano over the slices. Place them in the oven and bake for 20 minutes until they begin to brown. Turn them, sprinkle with the remaining chopped oregano, and bake for a further 5 minutes. Keep warm.

Cut the ciabatta bread into 12 ½-inch thick slices and place them on another baking sheet. Spread both sides with oil, then smear the top surface with half of the crushed garlic. Bake in the oven for 10 minutes until golden brown and crisp. Turn the slices over, smear them with the remainder of the garlic, and bake for a further 5 minutes.

Meanwhile, warm 1 tablespoon of olive oil with the honey in a skillet. Toss in the slices of prosciutto and cook for 5-6 minutes until curling and slightly crisp.

To assemble the crostini, place 2 eggplant circles side by side on each slice of baked bread, top with a curl of prosciutto, and garnish with oregano leaves.

Honey in Myth and Legend

Myths and legends about honey and bees are widespread throughout the world, and to some extent they still color the way we view the golden liquid and the insects which produce it.

By their very nature, legends are impossible to date, but the origins of many old tales must come from the earliest times of honey gathering. One of the enduring myths which was found in many cultures was that of honey signifying "truth." The Hebrew for bee is *dbure*, meaning word, so the bee has a mission to bring the Divine Word or truth. If, as was supposed, a bee alighted on the lips of Plato and St. Ambrose when they were children, then these men were sure to be blessed with truth and genius. Honey was put on newborn babies' lips in the hope of endowing them with wisdom and happiness – a custom which was followed in places as far apart as the Ivory Coast of Africa, Germany, and India. The Egyptians, too, saw honey as imparting this gift of truth, eating it at certain festivals and incanting "Sweet is the Truth" as they did so.

The ancient Greeks believed that honey was the first food, predating even the creation of the world. It was therefore seen as the food of the gods. The mighty god Zeus was brought up secretly in a cave by nursemaids, after his mother Rhea gave birth to him. The nursemaids, Amalthea and Melissa, fed him on milk and honey. (The name Melissa means "she who makes honey.") The Greeks also had their own patron-god of bees and beekeepers, named Aristaeus. This Arcadian shepherd was the son of Apollo and came from the island of Malta, once known as Melita, or island of honey. The legend of Aristaeus led to the belief that bees spontaneously generate – a view held until at least the seventeenth century, when scientists were able to explain the life cycle of the bee. The story tells how Aristaeus was deprived of his beloved bees after causing the deaths of the woman he loved and her husband. He made sacrifices, including four bulls, to atone for these deaths, and after several days "huge and trailing clouds of bees, that now in the treetops unite and hang like a bunch of grapes from the pliant branches" were seen coming from the animals.

There are many myths worldwide about the origins of bees. People could not understand how new bees were formed, never seeing the insects mate and not understanding that just one bee, the queen, was responsible for a whole colony of insects. In the Byzantine civilisation, bees were thought to be the reincarnations of souls of the dead who had returned to earth and were therefore revered, while the Maya Indians from Central America believed that the insects came from some wondrous hive in the center of the earth and flew from it like sparks spilling from a volcano.

TELLING THE BEES

Even in more modern times, it was believed that bees would thrive only in harmonious families, and in both England and North America, they were supposed to be included in family happenings. They were considered to be models of domestic peace and harmony and were also highly industrious workers, attributes to which most households aspired. "Telling the bees" was vitally important, whether it was good or bad news or simply everyday happenings. Bees had to be told of a death in the family or they would die, too. The bad news had to be given before sunrise on the following day for all to be well.

Sometimes a piece of funeral cake and a drink of wine was left by the hive after a funeral. The bees might also be formally invited to the funeral, or the beehives turned around as the coffin was carried out of the house past them; this was a practice commonly followed in Devon and observed in the eighteenth century. Country people, believing that the bees took part in seasonal feasts, gave them extra honey or sugar on New Year's Day and strewed salt as a general protection for the insects on Good Friday.

The tradition of passing on family news to the bees is evoked in this country rhyme:

**Marriage, birth or burying
News across the seas,
All your sad or marrying
You must tell the bees.**

54

This painting, entitled Venus with Cupid the Honey Thief, *by Lucas Cranach the Elder, shows a juvenile Cupid taking honeycomb oblivious to the bees around him. Cupid was the son of Venus and Mercury.*

The ancient Greeks found honey soporific. According to legend, Zeus gave his father a honey drink before tying him up and dethroning him.

The Honeymoon Period

A honeymoon, or honeymonth, was traditionally the month spent after a wedding, although it has now come to mean a special break taken by a couple after their marriage. Whether it simply signified a sweet and happy first month, or whether it was connected to rituals actually involving honey, is not clear. Many cultures used honey as part of the wedding ceremony. Hindu newlyweds were sometimes married in the presence of a bowl of honey, and as the groom kissed the bride, he would say to her, "Honey, this is honey, the speech of thy tongue is honey, in my mouth lives the honey of the bee, in my teeth lives peace."

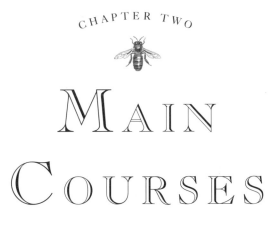

CHAPTER TWO

MAIN COURSES

I n almost every cuisine, there are main course recipes that show off the perfect marriage of sweet honey and meat. The honey is often used alongside fruits, spices, and herbs in such mouthwatering dishes as tagine of chicken and apricots, or sweet honey-glazed rack of lamb infused with the perfume of thyme.

Main Courses

Honey has always held an important place in culinary history, and modern life is becoming increasingly a rediscovery of the past. Honey-cured or glossy baked hams coated with honey and mustard are a throwback to medieval times, invoking images of banquets and suckling pigs. Many a medieval cook reached out for these alluring condiments to dress up an aging and tired piece of meat. From its prominent place in the kitchen and brewhouse, honey found its way into main-course dishes such as duck or ham, its sweetness mingling with the salty, sharp, and spicy flavors of ancient preservatives. Recipes using a combination of honey and fish, meat or poultry can sometimes have a cloying oversweetness, but this is countered particularly well by the sharpness of citrus fruits or the sourness of cherries or plums.

The Fishwife, *Adriaen van Ostrade, 1672*

Swarm

"A swarm of bees in May
Is worth a cow and a calf
that day;
A swarm of bees in June
Is worth a silver spoon;
A swarm of bees in July
Is not worth a butterfly."

TRADITIONAL IRISH
RHYME

WARM DUCK BREAST *with* MOROCCAN HONEY SAUCE

Inspired by the Moroccan fondness for honey, this exotically spiced crisp-skinned duck is perfectly matched by Couscous with Pistachios and Currants (page 80).

SERVES 4

1 cinnamon stick, halved	2tsp sugar
1tbsp strong hot black coffee	4 duck breasts with skin
¼tsp ground allspice	1 stick butter
¼tsp ground nutmeg	1¼ cups duck or chicken broth
4¼tbsp chestnut honey	

Place 1 piece of cinnamon stick in a shallow bowl, pour the hot coffee over it, and leave for 15 minutes to infuse. Remove the cinnamon stick and discard.

Place the allspice, nutmeg, cloves, 2 teaspoons of the honey, and sugar in a small bowl. Pour in the coffee and stir well to mix. Brush the mixture onto the skin of the duck breasts and leave for 2-3 hours to marinate. Set the remainder of the spiced marinade aside for the sauce.

Heat a heavy-based saucepan over a high heat until very hot. Place the marinated duck breasts in the pan, skin side down, and pan-fry for 5 minutes. Turn the breasts over and pan-fry for 2-3 minutes, then transfer to a baking sheet. Keep warm.

To make the sauce, pour all but 2 teaspoons of the duck fat from the pan. Add the butter. When this has melted, add the remainder of the marinade and pour in the broth. Add the remaining half of the cinnamon stick and the remaining honey. Simmer the liquid for about 8-10 minutes until it is reduced and clings to the back of a spoon. Remove the cinnamon stick and discard.

To serve, slice the duck breast into ¼-inch thick slices, arrange on large plates, and spoon the sauce over them.

60

HONEYED HAM
with a HERB CRUST

This succulent shoulder ham seasoned with honey and covered with a herb crust is based on the way the Romans would have cooked their ham in classical times. Try it as an evening meal with roasted vegetables or simply served with crusty bread and the mustard of your choice.

SERVES 4–6

3lb unsmoked shoulder ham	*1 sprig fresh rosemary plus*
6 cloves	*1tsp, roughly chopped*
¼tsp black peppercorns	*1 sprig fresh thyme plus ½tsp*
¼tsp green peppercorns	*roughly chopped*
3tbsp rosemary honey	*¾ cup fresh whole-wheat bread*
2 bay leaves	*crumbs*
2 sprigs parsley plus 1tbsp,	*1tbsp butter, melted*
roughly chopped	*freshly ground black pepper*

Place the ham in a large saucepan with the cloves, peppercorns, and 1 tablespoon of honey. Make a bunch of bouquet garni by tying together the bay leaves and the sprigs of parsley, rosemary, and thyme with string, then put the bouquet garni in the saucepan and cover with water. Bring the water to a boil and simmer for 45 minutes. Heat the oven to 375°F.

To make the herb crust, put the chopped parsley, rosemary, and thyme with the bread crumbs in a bowl and add 1 tablespoon of honey and the melted butter. Stir until mixed, then season with the black pepper and set aside until the ham is cooked.

Drain the ham and place it in a baking sheet, allowing it to cool slightly before snipping the string. Remove any fat from the top of the ham; then with a sharp knife make four incisions downward into the ham about 1 inch wide until the knife nearly reaches the base of the ham but doesn't cut through the bottom.

Place 1 teaspoon of honey in each incision, then press the crust firmly onto the ham until it is totally covered. Bake in the oven for 30 minutes until the crust is browned. Carve into slices with a sharp knife.

THAI SWEET *and* SOUR FISH

Baked whole, the succulent flesh of the fish is permeated with the flavors of the honey marinade; the process is assisted by three slits on each side of the fish. Honey is also used to flavor the accompanying chili dipping sauce. Serve with plain boiled rice tossed with fresh cilantro leaves and toasted cumin seeds.

SERVES 4

1 x 4½lb whole red snapper, or other whole white fish	*1 lime, juice only*
2 x 3in sticks lemon grass	*2 x 1in pieces cilantro root and stalk, chopped*
3 cloves garlic, 2 crushed, 1 peeled	*3½tbsp chopped fresh basil*
1in piece fresh ginger root, peeled and grated	*1 small bunch cilantro with roots*
1 large red chili pepper, roughly chopped	*½tsp coarse sea salt*
1 large green chili pepper, roughly chopped	*1½tsp crushed dried chili seeds*
	4tbsp lime blossom honey
	basil leaves for garnish

Heat the oven to 375°F.

Line a good-sized roasting pan with a piece of foil large enough to wrap around the fish. With a very sharp knife, make three diagonal cuts along each side of the fish.

To make the marinade, first remove and discard the tough outer leaves of one of the lemon grass sticks. Finely chop and place in a bowl with the crushed garlic, ginger, chili peppers, lime juice, chopped cilantro root, and basil. Mix them together well.

Place the crushed dried chili seeds and honey in a bowl with 6 tablespoons of warm water and stir until the honey is dissolved. Put 6 tablespoons of the mixture into a small bowl as a dipping sauce for serving.

To flavor the fish, spoon half of the remaining sweet chili sauce onto one side of the fish, then rub in half of the marinade. Turn the fish and repeat the process. Place the remaining lemon grass stick, cilantro, and whole garlic clove in the cavity of the fish. Sprinkle the fish with the sea salt, fold the foil over the fish, and seal.

Bake the fish in the oven for 15 minutes. Remove from the oven, undo the foil, and baste the fish with a few spoonfuls of the sauce. Reseal, return the fish to the oven, and bake for a further 10-15 minutes until cooked. The flesh should be bright white and flake away from the bone easily.

Serve on a large platter topped with basil leaves or cut each side of the fish into fillets and place, using a spatula, on individual plates. Serve accompanied by the sweet chili dipping sauce.

INDONESIAN SATAY SPARE RIBS

The combination of fragrant spices, honey, and peanuts gives this dish a real flavor of Indonesian food. The spare ribs can be served as finger food or as part of a sit-down meal garnished with cilantro leaves and accompanied by Crunchy Almond Noodles (page 81).

SERVES 4

3 cloves garlic, crushed	*1tsp sambal olek (chili paste)*
2 shallots, finely chopped	*1tbsp clear honey*
1tsp ground cumin	*2tbsp smooth peanut butter*
1tsp ground coriander	*1tbsp vegetable oil*
½tsp ground turmeric	*2lb pork spare ribs, on the bone*
½tsp chili powder	*cilantro leaves for garnish*
2tbsp ketjap manis (Indonesian soy sauce)	

In a bowl, mix the garlic, shallots, cumin, coriander, turmeric, and chili powder into a rough paste. Stir in the ketjap manis, sambal olek, honey, and peanut butter until well blended, then stir in the vegetable oil with 1 tablespoon of water to thin the paste slightly.

Arrange the spare ribs in a large shallow casserole dish. Using a pastry brush or the back of a teaspoon, spread the paste over them, turning them to completely cover. Place in the refrigerator and leave to marinate for at least 6 hours, or preferably overnight.

Heat a barbecue or broiler until hot and cook the spare ribs for 20-25 minutes until crisp and well-browned, turning them every 5 minutes.

Allow to cool slightly if serving as a finger food.

Spicy Pineapple Baby Chicken

Lime blossom honey and pineapple juice lend sweet and fruity overtones to these eastern spiced baby chickens. Excellent for a barbecue, they can also form part of an oriental meal made up of Chinese Stir-Fried Vegetables (page 85) or Crunchy Almond Noodles (page 81). Or they can be served with freshly boiled white or brown rice into which ¼ cup of the cooked marinade has been stirred.

SERVES 4

1¼ cups pure pineapple juice, unsweetened	6 small dried chili peppers, snipped
½ cup soy sauce	4tbsp lime blossom honey
¼ cup rice wine	4 baby chickens or poussin

Place all the ingredients except for the chicken in a large casserole dish and stir until well mixed. With a pair of poultry scissors or a sharp knife, cut the chicken in half down the backbone. Place in the refrigerator for 4-5 hours or overnight to marinate, turning the chicken halfway through.

Heat the oven to 375°F. Line a baking sheet with foil to prevent the marinade juices from baking onto the tray.

Remove the chicken from the marinade and place on the baking sheet. Bake in the oven for 30-35 minutes, basting occasionally with the marinade to improve the flavor and give a syrupy coating, until the chicken is cooked through and golden brown.

64

CRISPY LOIN *of* PORK *with* PLUM *and* ORANGE SAUCE

Following the centuries-old custom of flavoring pork and ham with honey, this succulent dish combines a traditional loin of pork with a contemporary sauce. The dish is also good served with Baked Honeyed Squash (page 78). If the plums are a bit tart, add an extra teaspoon of honey when you cook them.

SERVES 4

2½lb boned loin
   of pork with skin and fat,
   rolled and tied
4 fresh sage leaves
½tsp salt
SAUCE
¼ cup salted butter
6 ripe plums (about

10oz), roughly chopped
2½tbsp orange blossom honey
1 cup freshly squeezed orange
   juice
1 cup port wine
1½tbsp plum jam
1tbsp fresh sage, torn then
   roughly chopped

Heat the oven to 450°F.

Place the pork in a roasting pan. Push two whole sage leaves into each end of the roll. Rub the salt into the skin of the pork. Roast in the oven for 20 minutes, turn the heat down to 400°F and roast for a further 40-45 minutes, or until the liquid runs clear when the pork is pierced with a skewer.

Meanwhile, make the sauce. Melt the butter in a heavy-based skillet, then add the plums and honey. Cook for 3-5 minutes until the plums are beginning to soften.

Add the orange juice, port wine, and plum jam, bring to a boil, then reduce the heat and simmer for 25-30 minutes until the sauce is reduced to a syrupy consistency.

Remove the roast pork from the oven, slice off the crackling, and return it to the oven to crisp up further. Allow the pork to "rest" for 5-8 minutes before carving.

Meanwhile, toss the chopped sage into the sauce and reheat gently.

Slice the pork into ¼-inch circles then cut these across to make half circles. Overlap them on individual plates, spoon the reheated sauce over, and garnish with crackling.

CANTONESE SHREDDED BEEF

Stir-frying over high heat cooks food quickly while sealing in all the flavor. In this recipe, the beef is cooked until crisp and sweet. The flowery orange blossom honey counteracts the spiciness of the peppers while harmonizing with the sweetness of the carrots. The dish is best served with plain boiled rice to absorb the honeyed juices.

SERVES 4

2½tbsp sesame oil
3 cloves garlic, chopped
12 baby carrots cut into
   2in strips
1½tbsp soy sauce

6tbsp orange blossom honey
¼tsp chili powder or cayenne
   pepper
1lb beef filet, cut into thin strips
   2in long
¼tsp salt

In a wok or non-stick skillet, heat the oil until hot. Add the garlic and cook until it is just turning golden.

Add the carrots with 2 teaspoons of soy sauce, 1 tablespoon of honey, and ¼ teaspoon of chili powder or cayenne pepper and stir-fry for 2-3 minutes until the carrots are just starting to soften.

Add the beef with the remainder of the soy sauce, honey, chili powder or cayenne pepper, and the salt. Stir-fry for a further 5-7 minutes until the beef is a dark golden brown and slightly crispy and the carrots are caramelized. Serve immediately.

65

Orange Blossom

Honey made from orange blossom can lend a distinctive flavor to a recipe as in Crispy Loin of Pork (left), but oranges themselves also have a natural affinity with honey. The sugar that makes honey sweet highlights the zest of the orange. Traditionally orange complements honey in sweet dishes, such as baklava, the Greek honey spiced cake, and savory ones such as duck, where the citric acid orange helps to counteract the natural fattiness of the bird.

Performing Bees

One of the most unusually sited beehives is the one positioned on the roof of the Paris Opéra. Established in 1984 by Jean Paucton, a backstage worker in charge of set furniture, the hive produces a strong-tasting honey some people find overpowering. This unique flavor is due to the huge variety of flowers from which the Opéra bees gather their nectar. Free to roam all over Paris, they visit flowers on the boulevards and balconies, in the large open parks, and even the Père-Lachaise Cemetery. And since the city is usually several degrees warmer than the outlying rural areas, flowers bloom earlier and so the urban bees have a longer honey-making season. The fruits of their labors are on sale, at a premium price, in the souvenir shop of the Opéra itself, and at Fauchon (above), the prestigious Paris food store.

Another French institution to have a link with beehives is the Comédie-Française, the prestigious theater company founded by Louis

XIV in 1680. The beehive was felt to be an appropriate symbol for an acting troupe, since it represents individual effort by the many for the good of the whole. This modern souvenir chocolate coin carrying the beehive was produced as a memento of the money traditionally thrown as tokens of appreciation at the unpaid actors early in the history of the company.

RACKS *of* LAMB *with a* THYME *and* HONEY GLAZE

The use of thyme honey in this recipe cleverly links a traditional method of glazing meat with the subtle flavoring of fresh herbs. The result is handsome enough for an elegant dinner and particularly well matched in flavor to the Shallot Confit on page 86. Leaving on any excess fat enhances the flavor of the dish.

SERVES 4

4 racks of lamb, each with 4 cutlets (about 2lb)	2tbsp thyme honey
2 cloves garlic, halved	1tbsp fresh thyme leaves, stripped from the stems
1tsp yellow mustard seeds	sprigs of thyme for garnish

Heat the oven to 400°F.

Lay the racks of lamb flat in a roasting pan with the bones touching the base and rub the flesh all over with the cut ends of the garlic cloves. Crush the garlic cloves and place in a bowl.

Using a pestle and mortar, crush the mustard seeds until they are just split open. Add the split seeds with the honey to the garlic and stir well, mixing all the ingredients evenly.

Spread the mixture over the back of the racks of lamb, then sprinkle with the thyme leaves. Place immediately in the oven and bake for 15 minutes to crisp up the fat. Turn the heat down to 350°F and roast for a further 20 minutes, or until the liquid runs clear when the lamb is pierced with a skewer.

Serve the racks whole, garnished with sprigs of thyme.

Peas & Honey

"I eat my peas with honey,
I've done it all my life,
It makes my peas taste funny,
But it keeps them on my knife."

ANON.

Chestnuts

Chestnut honey is made from the blossom of the sweet or Spanish chestnut, which is sometimes known in England as the "breadfruit tree" (not to be confused with the tropical breadfruit tree grown in the South Pacific) because it provides man with so much for free. The nuts can be eaten fresh in soups, casseroles, stuffings, and pies, often bulking out scarce and expensive meat; they can be dried for use in cooking or ground to a flour for making breads and batters, or they may be candied. Even the leaves can be used as winter feed for cattle.

TAGINE *of* CHICKEN *with* APRICOTS *and* PRUNES

A tagine is a traditional Moroccan stew cooked very slowly in an earthenware pot (also called a tagine). This method of cooking allows the meat to absorb all the flavors. Chestnut honey contributes a rich, nutty sweetness to this chicken version which is emphasized by the honeyed apricots, although ordinary dried apricots will do. Serve the tagine on a bed of couscous to soak up the juices.

SERVES 4

2tbsp butter	*3lb chicken, cut into*
3tbsp vegetable oil	*8 pieces*
2 cloves garlic	*12 shallots, peeled*
pinch saffron	*3oz honeyed dried apricots*
½tsp cayenne pepper	*4oz prunes*
⅛tsp finely ground black pepper	*1tbsp chestnut honey*
½tsp crushed coriander seeds	*¼tsp ground cinnamon*
¼tsp ground ginger	

Melt the butter in a large saucepan or casserole dish, then add the oil and heat. Add the garlic, a good pinch of saffron, the cayenne pepper, black pepper, crushed coriander seeds, and ginger and saute everything together for 1-2 minutes. Add the chicken pieces, toss them in the spice mixture to cover them well, and cook for 3-4 minutes to allow the spices to penetrate.

Add enough water to the pan or casserole dish to almost cover the chicken. Bring to a boil, then simmer for 45-50 minutes, covered. Add the shallots and cook for another 20 minutes, uncovered.

After 20 minutes, add the apricots, prunes, honey, and cinnamon, then continue to cook for 30 minutes until the sauce has reduced and the chicken is almost falling off the bone. The dish can be served immediately, but its rich flavors will improve if it is made in advance and stored, covered, in the refrigerator for a couple of days.

68

Brewing Honey

Mead and metheglin are both fermented honey-based drinks, the difference between them being that mead simply consists of fermented honey and water with no additional flavorings, while metheglin is flavored with spices and sometimes herbs. It is not uncommon, though, to come across versions that do not conform to this purist distinction. Mead has been brewed worldwide since very early times, and, according to legend, was drunk by Dionysius and Bacchus before the grapevine was cultivated. Records show that mead had become popular in England by 334 B.C., and it remained a staple drink in England and other northern European countries until the nineteenth century, when a decline in bee numbers led to an increase in the price of honey. But mead continued to be brewed on a small scale and is still produced today.

Old Sussex Recipe *for* Mead

Take 6 pounds of any light floral honey and put it into a big pot with 10 quarts of water, rainwater if possible, and heat until boiling. Add spices you like best such as cinnamon, ginger, cloves, or nutmeg. Then reduce over a gentle heat until only 6 pints of liquid remain. Pour the liquid into pottery or earthenware pots and allow to cool. Add about 1 ounce of fresh yeast and leave to ferment for 3 days. When fermentation is over, pour into casks, or bottles, and keep for a year before drinking.

Queen Elizabeth's Metheglin

First, gather a bushel of sweetbriar leaves, and a bushel of thyme, half a bushel of rosemary, and a peck of bay leaves. Seethe all these, being well-washed, in a furnace not less than 120 gallons, of fair water. Let them boil the space of half an hour or better, and then pour out all the water and herbs into a vat. Let it stand until it be but milk warm, then strain the water from the herbs, and take to every six gallons of water, one gallon of the finest honey, and put it into the boorne. Labour it together half an hour, then let it stand for two days, stirring it well twice or thrice each day. Then take the liquor and boil it anew, and when it does seethe, skim it as long as there remains any dross. When it is clear, put it into a vat as before, and there let it be cooled. You must then have in readiness a kive of new ale or beer, which as soon as you have emptied, suddenly whelm it upside down, and set it up again, and presently put in the metheglin, and let it stand three days a-working. And then turn it up in barrels, tying at every taphole (by a pack thread) a little bag of beaten cloves and mace, to the value of an ounce. Leave for half a year before drinking.

Strong Honey Ale

Honey can also be added to hop-based brews. As well as reducing the bitterness of the hops, the flavor of the honey adds a unique roundness. This ale can be very strong and should only be drunk in moderation!

MAKES 1¼ GALLONS

20oz pure malt extract	1½ cups pure apple juice
10oz clear honey	1 sachet ale yeast
1¼oz Goldings hops	

YOU WILL ALSO NEED: Chempro SDP or solution of sodium metabisulfite; large plastic container with lid (holding at least 2 gallons) for fermenting; long plastic spoon or spatula; wine or beer hydrometer; plastic bottles.

Put about 2 pints of cold water in a large stainless steel pan over medium heat. Stir in the malt extract, honey, and apple juice using a plastic spoon or spatula. Bring to a boil and add 1 ounce of the hops to this mixture. Stir well, cover partially, and boil steadily but not too vigorously for 45 minutes, stirring occasionally to beat back the hops. After 45 minutes, stir in the remaining ¼ ounce of hops and boil steadily for another 15–20 minutes. Turn off the heat.

Sterilize the large plastic container, the lid, and the plastic spoon or spatula, rinse carefully with cold water and drain. Now strain the liquid into the fermenting vessel and top it up with cold water to 1¼ gallons. Stir vigorously to aerate, cover, and cool to room temperature. When cool, add the contents of the yeast sachet, cover and store in a warm place until fermentation is complete. Check this by measuring the specific gravity with a sterilized hydrometer until the reading stays constant for a couple of days. Fermentation takes from 3 to 5 days.

When fermentation is complete, sterilize, rinse, and drain the required number of bottles and tops. Fill each bottle to within about 2 inches of the top and seal. Store the bottles in a warm place for about 5 days. Check that not too much pressure is building up in the bottles and unscrew the tops to release excess pressure if necessary, sealing them up again. After 5 days, move the bottles to a cool, dark place and leave to mature for at least 3 months. When ready, decant the ale into another container before drinking, taking care not to disturb the yeast sediment.

Honey Pots

*While honey's main culinary purpose in the past was
as an ingredient for cooking and brewing, it is more
likely to appear on today's table as a spread or
sweetener for cereals or desserts. Afternoon tea may be
on the decline, with fewer occasions to spread honey
on slices of fresh bread and butter, or toasted muffins,
but we still buy plenty of the stuff, and many of us
decant it from its jar into a special honey pot. In the
Victorian and Edwardian days of long, leisurely
breakfasts and teas served by the fire in the drawing
room, it was commonplace to have a choice of
homemade jams, spicy spreads, marmalades, and
honeys. Silver, china, or cut-glass pots and jars were
specially made to hold the many different flavors of
jam and honey.*

*Honey pots have always captured the imagination of
designers, given that the world of bees, hives, and
honeycombs offer so many wonderful visual references
to inspire them. The skep and hive were favorite
shapes to make into pots – complete with lids, of
course, and a space to hold a spoon or special honey
drizzler. Honey might be poured from its original jar
into the decorative one or, if the decorative container
was large enough and the right shape, a complete jar
of honey could be stood inside it. Special honey spoons
were marketed with a little hook halfway up their
stem. After using it to put honey on your slice of
bread, the spoon was hooked over the jar edge to
drain. Why this was seen as necessary is a slight
mystery, but it was presumably to save the risk of
sticky fingers if the spoon slipped lower into the liquid
honey. The 1930s and 1950s saw a rise in the
popularity of inexpensive, novelty tea sets and
other china, which were often elaborately
molded and highly decorated. Honey pots were
a favorite choice for mass production, especially
to be sold as souvenirs. In Britain, tea was still
an important family meal; for many it was the main
meal of the day. It included a hot dish followed by
bread and butter and cakes, washed down with tea. A
quirky china honey pot was just the thing to brighten
up the table.*

1. *This Roman honey jar is made
from glazed clay. Presumably
parchment or skin would have been
tied over the top if the honey was to
have been stored for any length of time.
The handles made it easy to carry, as
honey was an important sacrifice to
various gods and had to be transported
to temples and shrines.*

2. *This elaborate
and ornate ink stand
takes the beehive as its
design starting point.
Made from ormolu
and bronze, the four
lotus shapes
around the hive
are for holding
pens.*

4. *This china honey pot is a slightly unusual shape, but still appears to be based on a straw skep. It has a stand and lid decorated with large molded leaves and dates from around 1730.*

3. *The bee skep shape was the most obvious and enduring inspiration for honey-pot makers. This one made from glass was originally decorated, but the color has worn away with constant use.*

7. *These mass-produced ceramic pots from the 1950s are in the chunky style typical of the decade. The images used, of a skep and a honeycomb, are perennially popular.*

5. *This honey pot is made from Faience and dates from the eighteenth century. Peasant pottery of this type is generally brightly decorated in this bold style, and the blue, green, and yellow design showing a woman picking flowers is very typical.*

8. *One of a pair of small but highly detailed English silver honey pots and stands which date from the time of George III are based on a straw skep shape.*

6. *This pale yellow glass honey pot was made in Somerset between 1830 and 1840. It is easy to imagine it on a gracious early Victorian tea table among fine bone china tea services and elegant silver.*

CHAPTER THREE

VEGETABLES

 hint of honey can do surprising things for everyday and more unusual vegetables and accompaniments, from rich wintry spiced red cabbage to light fluffy couscous studded with nuts and dried fruit. Root vegetables, no matter how sweet they are, always benefit from a touch of honey as well.

VEGETABLES

Vegetables are an integral part of a meal, so why treat them as an afterthought? Many have a sweetish tinge, which is enhanced by a little honey. But take care not to smother their natural sweetness with overpowering flavors. More robust vegetables, like squash or fennel, cope well with unusual or powerful flavors. Their vast range of textures and colors make vegetables ideal for exciting stir-fry dishes, perhaps combined with honey, ginger, and plenty of garlic. Rice, the staple diet of most of the world, and other grains have a natural blandness which is transformed magically by subtle blends of herbs, spices, and honey. Honey is also perfect for fruit or vegetable confits, with their combination of sweet and sour flavors. With the increasing availability of exciting and exotic vegetables from all over the world and a growing trend toward meals based around vegetables and legumes, these recipes represent many styles and cultures, both classic and innovative.

*Fresco of a vegetable market from Issogno
Castle, Valle Aosta, Italy, fiftennth century*

RED CABBAGE TOSSED *in* HONEY *and* CARAWAY

Adapted from traditional German recipes for red cabbage, this version is made sweeter by the addition of honey. Balsamic vinegar, a mild, intensely fragrant wine vinegar, is kinder to the honey than a more traditional, harsher type would be. The dish goes well with Crispy Loin of Pork (page 64). Caraway seeds can be toasted by stirring them around a hot skillet for about 1 minute.

SERVES 4

1 red cabbage (about 1lb)
¼ cup salted butter
1 onion, sliced
½ cup golden raisins

1½tbsp clover honey
1tbsp balsamic vinegar or other
    red wine vinegar
½tsp caraway seeds, toasted

Using a large, sharp knife, cut the cabbage into ½-inch shreds. In a large saucepan, melt the butter and sauté the onion over a medium heat for 2-3 minutes until transparent.

Add the raisins to the pan and toss through the butter. Stir in the honey, mixing well. Add the shredded cabbage and the balsamic vinegar. Stir in the toasted caraway seeds until mixed through.

Turn the heat down to low, cover and steam the red cabbage for 10-15 minutes until it is tender, tossing once or twice with tongs during the cooking time. Serve immediately.

BAKED HONEYED SQUASH

This caramelized squash melts in the mouth and makes a scrumptious accompaniment to poultry and meat dishes. It is especially good with Racks of Lamb with a Thyme and Honey Glaze (page 67). If you cannot find butternut squash, substitute any other orange squash or pumpkin.

SERVES 4

1lb butternut squash, deseeded
2tbsp salted butter

1tbsp creamy honey, warmed
½tsp chopped fresh rosemary,
    or ¼tsp dried rosemary

Heat the oven to 375°F.

Cut the squash into ¼-inch circles and cut these in half to make half circles. Place the squash pieces in a bowl with the warmed honey and toss to coat well.

Arrange the squash, overlapping the pieces, in a roasting pan or large shallow ovenproof dish. Drizzle the honey syrup left in the bowl over the squash. Dot the squash with the butter, then sprinkle with the rosemary.

Bake in the oven for 30-35 minutes until golden brown and caramelized.

Sing a Song of Sixpence

*"The king was in his counting-house
Counting out his money
The queen was in the parlor
Eating bread and honey."*

TRADITIONAL NURSERY RHYME

Couscous *with* Pistachios *and* Currants

Any spiced meat or poultry would be enhanced by this sweet, nutty variation of the classic Moroccan couscous. It is particularly good as an accompaniment to Warm Duck Breast with Moroccan Sauce (page 60).

SERVES 4

10oz couscous	1/3 cup raisins
1/3 cup butter	1¾tbsp lime blossom honey
1/2 cup pistachios, shelled	

Place the couscous in a large bowl and pour over 1 cup boiling water. Stir thoroughly and leave for about 5 minutes to allow the grains to absorb the water and swell.

Melt the butter in a large skillet, then add the pistachios and raisins. Cook for 2 minutes until the nuts begin to crisp, then add the honey and cook for a further 1-2 minutes. Add the soaked couscous and stir through for 2-3 minutes until well mixed and coated with butter and honey.

CRUNCHY ALMOND NOODLES

Although honey is not often used in Chinese cuisine, the inclusion of fragrant orange blossom honey in this recipe introduces a pleasing sweet element to a traditional dish. Noodles are one of the staples of Far Eastern cooking; there, they are eaten at least once a day.

SERVES 4

¼ cup flaked almonds
6oz Chinese thread egg noodles
2tbsp sesame oil
1tbsp thick soy sauce
2tbsp orange blossom honey
2tbsp chives, snipped
   into 2in lengths

Heat the oven to 400°F.

Put the flaked almonds on a baking sheet and place them in the oven for 3-5 minutes until golden. Remove and allow to cool.

Cook the noodles in a saucepan of boiling water, then drain. Pour the sesame oil and soy sauce into the same saucepan and add the honey. Return the noodles to the saucepan and toss gently to coat them evenly. Add the snipped chives and toss again. Finally, add the almonds, toss through, and serve immediately.

If you work quickly during the last stages of preparation, the noodles should retain their heat; should you need to reheat them, either set the saucepan over a very low heat or place the noodles in the microwave on high for 30-40 seconds.

GINGERED HONEY CARROTS

Sweet, honeyed carrots flavored with the distinctive taste of freshly toasted cumin seeds take only a little more time to prepare than ordinary steamed carrots but have double the flavor. Cumin seeds can be toasted by stirring them around a hot skillet for about 1 minute.

SERVES 4

¼ cup butter
8 carrots (about 1lb), cut into
 sticks about 3in long by
 ¼in wide

2in piece fresh gingerroot,
 peeled and cut
 into thin strips
1tbsp acacia honey
½tsp cumin seeds, toasted

Melt the butter in a large skillet, add the carrots and the ginger, and sauté for 2-3 minutes.

Add the honey and cook for a further 4-5 minutes until the carrots are tender but still firm. Add the toasted cumin seeds, toss thoroughly, and warm through for 1 minute before serving.

Honey Lovers

Before man created purpose-built hives, bears developed various strategies to rob bees of their precious honey, such as waiting until night before knocking down a hive suspended from the underside of a rock. In the darkness, the bees tended to buzz around the site of the comb rather than attack the marauder.

Nowadays bears must adapt their honey-hunting skills to cope with man-made hives, sometimes protected in apiaries by an electric fence.

BAKED HONEY BEETS

The unique flavor of beets is superbly matched by the sweetness of honey. Because it is cooked in an oven, this dish makes an ideal accompaniment for roasts.

SERVES 4

1tbsp creamy honey
1tsp olive oil
8 baby beets (about

13oz), uncooked
¼tsp finely ground black pepper

Heat the oven to 375°F.

In a bowl large enough to hold all the beets, mix together the honey and the oil until blended.

Peel each beet and place in the bowl with the honey mixture. Toss the beets in the honey mixture, then sprinkle with black pepper.

Place the beets in a casserole dish and drizzle any excess honey mixture over them. Bake in the oven for 35-40 minutes, turning the beets twice during the cooking time.

CHINESE STIR-FRIED VEGETABLES *with* HONEY *and* SESAME SEEDS

Honey and sesame seeds enhance the natural flavors of the crisp, stir-fried vegetables. The principle of stir-frying is to allow food to be cooked quickly before it loses any of its goodness or taste; a wok is specially shaped for this style of cooking, but a heavy-bottomed skillet will do.

SERVES 4

2tbsp sesame oil
2 cloves garlic, roughly chopped
1 yellow sweet pepper,
  cut into thin strips
8 scallions, cut on the diagonal
  into 1in strips
1 cup sugar snap peas

1 cup beansprouts
7oz pak choi (Chinese cabbage),
  trimmed, leaves left whole
1½tbsp sesame seeds
1½tbsp soy sauce
1½tbsp acacia honey

In a wok or heavy-bottomed skillet, heat the sesame oil over medium-high heat. When it is hot, add the garlic and sweet pepper and stir-fry until the pepper just begins to brown around the edges.

Add the scallions and sugar snap peas and stir-fry for 1-2 minutes.

Add the bean sprouts, pak choi, sesame seeds, soy sauce, and honey and stir-fry for a further 2-3 minutes. Serve immediately.

SHALLOT CONFIT

With the consistency of chutney or marmalade, this confit is superb with meats and strong cheeses. The confit can be eaten warm; alternatively, it can be kept in a sealed jar in the refrigerator for up to one week and eaten cold.

SERVES 4

20 shallots (about 1lb), peeled	4tbsp white wine vinegar
1 leek, sliced	2½tbsp clear honey
¼ cup raisins	2½tbsp olive oil

Combine all the ingredients in a small saucepan. Place over a medium heat and bring to a boil.

Simmer over a low heat for 1¼ hours, or until the liquid has reduced and thickened to become syrupy. Keep a watchful eye on the heat during the simmering; if the heat is too high, the syrup may burn. Allow the confit to cool slightly before serving.

Try shallot confit with Stilton or Roquefort cheese, or some cold slices of roast beef or lamb for a Mediterranean-style plowman's lunch.

Shalot.
Confit.

1	2	3
9	10	4
8	7 6	5

This illustration, *taken from* Graphic Illustrations of Animals, Showing their Utility to Man, *beautifully illustrates the myriad and varied benefits we gain from the bee. In the form of honey, it provides a basic food stuff and a medical remedy (1 and 5), while beeswax gives us light in the form of candles (3 and 4). Certain species of animals and birds rely on honey as a food source; here African tribemen follow ratels in order to locate honey for themselves (6). Other, more marginal benefits come in the form of wax flowers and wax museums (8 and 9). And from this picture (7) it would appear that bees have even been used as a weapon of war! However, we have a particular reason to be seriously grateful to the honeybee (2 and 10). It has been calculated that if bees were to become extinct, not only garden flowers but world crops would fail through lack of pollination. Deprived of food sources, we would not survive for more than two years.*

88

Food

Ornamental Industry.

WAX FLOWERS

Wax Models.

S. Europe.

Worker

American

Indian.

Published by T.

Defence made with Bees.

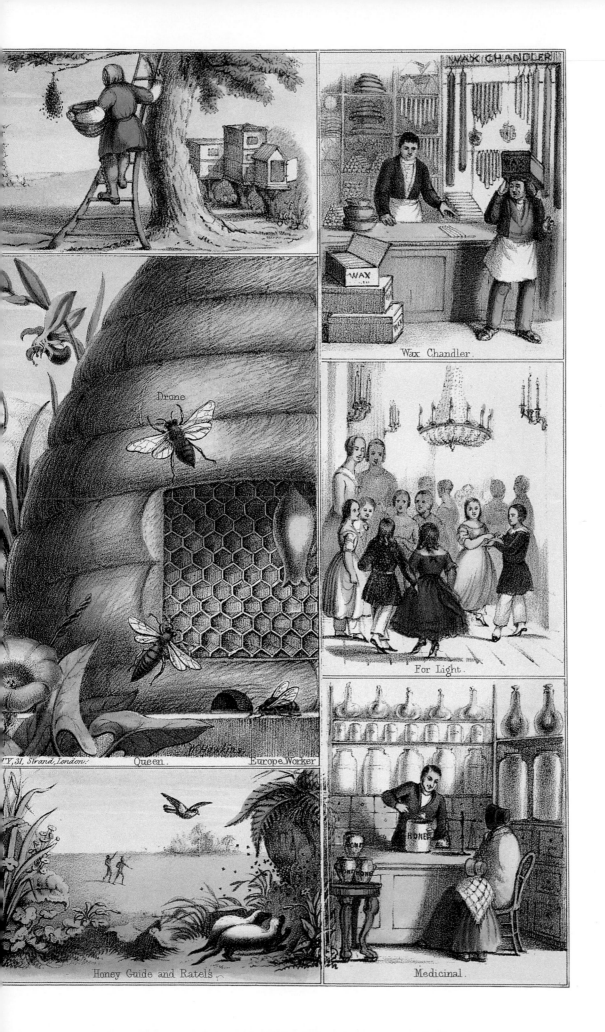

Wax Chandler.

For Light.

Medicinal.

Honey Guide and Ratels.

Drone.

Queen.

Europe Worker.

W. Hawkins.

TY, 31, Strand, London.

89

CHAPTER FOUR

DESSERTS

Because honey blends so perfectly with so many fresh and dried fruits, its inclusion can make fruit-based desserts even more delectable. It makes smooth and creamy puddings even more alluring, and its hints of flower fragrances and mild sweetness enhance delicious delicate desserts, such as mousses and syllabubs.

DESSERTS

Ambrosia was the original food of the gods, and we still use the word ambrosial for foods, particularly desserts, that are so delicious they hint at the divine. Honey really excells when it comes to desserts. More intensely sweet than the equivalent amount of sugar, it makes an ideal sweetening agent; whether liquid or set, it mixes easily and quickly with other ingredients.

Perfect in dishes including cream and yogurt which will not be heated, it leaves no gritty texture as sugar would. And, in addition to sweetness, it provides its own unique flavor, experienced at its best in simple dishes. Try thick Greek yogurt drizzled with a dark, powerfully scented honey such as Greek mountain honey for a perfect marriage of flavors.

La Pâtisserie Gloppe aux Champs Elysées, *Jean Beraud, 1889*

LAVENDER HONEY CHEESECAKE

Flavored with lavender flowers and lavender honey, this delicious cheesecake evokes a hot, peaceful summer's day full of the sound of bees buzzing over clumps of heady blossom. If you use dried lavender, make sure it is organically dried and contains no coloring agents. You can decorate the cheesecake with crystallized lavender stems: dip stems in egg white, then immediately in superfine sugar, and place them on a wire cooling rack to dry.

SERVES 6–8

½ lb Scottish shortbread cookies	*6oz lavender honey*
5tbsp butter, melted	*8oz light soft cheese*
3tbsp lavender petals, fresh or dried, tied in cheesecloth	*1¼ cups heavy cream*

For the base, place the shortbread cookies in a plastic bag and crush them until quite fine using a rolling pin. Place the crumbs in a bowl and stir in the melted butter. Press this mixture into a 9-inch springform cake pan using the back of a large metal spoon, and place in the refrigerator for 1 hour.

To make the lavender infusion, pour 2½ tablespoons of boiling water into a small bowl with 2 teaspoons of the lavender honey. Place the cheesecloth sachet of lavender petals in the bowl and leave for 15 minutes to infuse. Remove the sachet and let the water cool.

In a large bowl, beat together the light soft cheese and the remainder of the honey until smooth, then gradually add the lavender water until it is absorbed and the mixture is light and smooth. Whip the cream until it forms soft peaks and gently fold it into the soft cheese mixture. Pour the filling over the crumb base; then place in the refrigerator for 3-4 hours until set.

Before serving the cheesecake, run a warm knife around the edge of the springform pan. Slice to serve.

TOFFEE APPLES *with* HONEY ICE CREAM

This delicious honey ice-cream made with fragrant heather honey is quick and simple to prepare. It is quite divine served with caramelized apple.

SERVES 4

2 large crisp green eating apples (about 12oz)	ICE CREAM
	2 eggs
2tbsp salted butter	*4tbsp heather honey*
2tbsp heather honey	*2½ cups heavy cream*
7tbsp cognac	

First make the ice cream. In a bowl beat together the eggs, honey, and cream until well blended. Pour the mixture into a small saucepan and heat over a low heat, stirring constantly until warm to the touch. Be careful not to overcook as the eggs will start to scramble if you do. Allow to cool.

Pour the ice-cream mixture into four small molds and place in the freezer for at least 3-4 hours until frozen solid.

Decore the apples and cut them into quarters, leaving the skins on. Slice the quarters wafer thin.

Melt the butter in a large skillet, add the apples and sauté for 3-4 minutes. Add the honey and cognac and heat until bubbling. Continue to cook over a medium-high heat for 15-20 minutes until the mixture is a rich golden brown. Keep warm.

Remove the ice-cream from the molds. Hold the base of each mold carefully under running cold water, then run a knife around the edges to loosen the ice cream. Place on to a large, flat dinner plate and allow to soften for 3-4 minutes. Spoon the warm toffeed apples on one side and serve immediately.

Mrs. Beeton

Mrs. Beeton's Book of Household Management, *published in 1861, is recognized all over the world as an all-time cookbook classic today. One of its most fascinating aspects is its insight into historical uses of and attitudes to food.*

At the time Mrs. Beeton was writing, white sugar was the cheapest, and therefore the most popular, sweetening. However, she recognized the advantages of honey and used it for its preservative qualities: in a sweet loaf of bread so that it would keep well and to make a distinctively flavored honey pudding. She also produced an orange marmalade that contained honey.

LIME *and* HONEY GRANITA

Like other sharp-tasting water ices, this granita can be used as a between-course palate cleanser or simply as a welcome refresher on a hot day. The lime honey complements the slightly tingling freshness of the champagne. The granita mixture can be kept for up to one week in an airtight container in the freezer.

SERVES 4

3 limes, chopped flesh and any juice plus zest for decoration
3½ tbsp lime blossom honey

1¼ cups champagne or sparkling wine, at room temperature

Beat the lime and the honey together in a bowl until they are well blended.

Pour the champagne or sparkling wine into the bowl, beating constantly. When the honey is dissolved, pour the mixture into a shallow tray that will not mark when scraped with a fork. Place in the freezer for 7-8 hours or overnight.

Remove the tray from the freezer and, using a fork, crush

the ice mixture to break it up. Place the granita in the freezer for at least 2-3 hours and serve decorated with lime zest.

97

HONEY *and* MADEIRA SYLLABUB

Syllabubs are old favorites, but this one has been given a new twist. Serve it straight from the refrigerator; if left standing at room temperature for too long, liquid will collect at the bottom of the glass or bowl. Whipping the cream in a chilled bowl will thicken it and help it to hold its shape.

SERVES 4

1¼ cups heavy cream
2 tbsp Canadian clover honey
¾ cup madeira wine

2 tbsp flaked almonds
12 savioardi biscuits (Italian finger cookies)

Heat the oven to 400°F.

Place the cream in a chilled ceramic bowl or over ice and whip for 15-20 seconds until slightly thick.

Add the honey and beat for a further 10 seconds. Pour a continuous stream of madeira wine into the cream and honey, beating continuously until it is absorbed. Continue to beat until the mixture is thick enough to form gentle peaks. Spoon into individual serving glasses or a single bowl and chill in the refrigerator for 2½-3 hours.

Place the flaked almonds on a baking sheet and place in the oven for 3-5 minutes until golden brown. Remove and allow to cool.

Serve the syllabub sprinkled with the roasted almonds and the savioardi biscuits on the side.

TARTLETS *of* DRIED FRUITS

Made with festive fruits and a honeyed custard, these delicate, reassuringly old-fashioned tarts with highly layered puff pastry sides are at once light and sinful.

SERVES 4

2tbsp raisins
1tbsp golden raisins
1tbsp mixed candied peel
2tsp sugar
½tsp ground allspice, plus
    a little for sprinkling

1 egg
1¼ cups heavy cream
1½tsp orange blossom honey
2 x 12x8in sheets ready-made
    puff pastry (about 8oz)

Place the raisins, golden raisins, candied peel, sugar, and ¼ teaspoon of the allspice in a bowl. Cover with warm water, then leave for 30-40 minutes until the dried fruits are re-hydrated and plumped up.

To make the honey custard, beat the egg, then add ¾ cup of the cream, the remaining ¼ teaspoon of allspice, and the honey. Set aside.

Drain the rehydrated dried fruit in a colander and leave the fruit in the colander over a bowl.

Select four 4-inch tart pans and cut out circles from the puff pastry sheets using a pastry cutter about 2 inches wider than the pans; alternatively, use an appropriately sized upturned glass and cut around the rim with a small, sharp knife. Line the ungreased pans with the pastry circles (the high butter content of the puff pastry makes greasing unnecessary) and trim off the overlap. Holding a small,

sharp knife with the blade pointing upright and facing toward your body, gently slice away the excess pastry without dragging the knife.

Refrigerate the pastry-lined tart pans for 20-25 minutes. Heat the oven to 400°F.

Arrange the well-drained dried fruit on the bottom of the pastry cups and pour over the honey custard to almost fill them. Sprinkle on a little allspice. Bake the tarts in the oven for 25-30 minutes until golden brown.

Meanwhile, whip the remainder of the heavy cream in a chilled bowl and place in the refrigerator until needed.

Remove the cooked tarts from the oven and allow to cool for 2-3 minutes. To serve, place each tart on a dinner plate, sprinkle with allspice, and spoon a portion of cream to one side.

The Owl and the Pussy Cat

"The Owl and the Pussy-Cat went to sea
In a beautiful pea-green boat
They took some honey, and plenty of money,
Wrapped up in a five-pound note."

NONSENSE SONGS, EDWARD LEAR 1812–88

GREEK HONEYED FIGS
with RICH YOGURT

There can be no better way of serving fresh figs than simply prepared with honey and Greek-style yogurt. They are opened out, briefly baked, and served on delicate squares of crisp phyllo pastry. The fresher the figs, the better.

SERVES 4

8 fresh figs with stems	*into 4 squares about*
2 cinnamon sticks, each broken	*4x3in*
into 4 pieces	*1tsp ground cinnamon*
3tbsp Greek mountain honey	*½ cup Greek-style yogurt*
2 sheets phyllo pastry, each cut	

Heat the oven to 375°F.

Carefully cut the figs in half from the base to just below the stem, keeping them joined at the stem. Place the figs, opened flat and skin side down, in a large ovenproof dish and arrange the cinnamon pieces around them.

Drizzle the honey over the figs and bake them in the oven for 25-30 minutes, basting the figs every 10 minutes.

Arrange the pastry squares in one layer on a baking sheet. Remove the baked figs from the oven. Place the pastry in the oven and bake for 3-4 minutes until golden brown.

To serve, dust four plates with ground cinnamon, arrange 2 pastry squares on each, and top each square with 1 opened-out fig. Spoon a portion of yogurt on one side.

WHISKEY, HONEY, *and* CARDAMOM CAKES

A classic combination, whiskey and honey work well together in this comforting dessert. Although cooked in the oven, the cakes are surprisingly moist.

SERVES 4

3tbsp whole milk	*5tbsp eucalyptus honey*
¼ cup salted butter, plus extra for greasing	*2 eggs*
	4tbsp whiskey
1 cup self-rising flour	*1 cup extra thick heavy cream*
1tsp ground cinnamon	
4 pods of cardamom seeds	SYRUP
4 clove heads, the small round part attached to the stalk	*2tbsp whiskey*
	2tbsp eucalyptus honey
½ cup light brown sugar	

Heat the oven to 350°F.

Warm the milk in a small saucepan, then melt the butter in it. Allow to cool.

Sift the flour with the cinnamon into a bowl. Crush the cardamom pods and cloves using a mortar and pestle and sprinkle onto the sifted flour.

In a separate bowl, mix the brown sugar, 4 tablespoons of the honey, and the eggs until smooth, then stir in the whiskey and the milk and butter mixture.

Make a well in the center of the flour with a spoon and gradually pour in the whiskey and honey mixture, about 6 tablespoons at a time and whipping slowly with a fork to gently incorporate the flour. When all the flour is incorporated, the mixture should have the consistency of a smooth, thick batter.

Pour the mixture into four greased ½ cup molds or pans; do not fill to the brim as the mixture will rise during baking. Place in the oven and bake for 20-25 minutes; the cakes are cooked through when a skewer comes out clean. Remove from the oven and allow to cool.

Trim the puffed-up tops slightly so that they will sit evenly and unmold them into a casserole or baking dish, trimmed side down.

Mix the syrup ingredients together and spoon over the cakes until they are saturated and leave them to soak through for 1-2 hours.

When ready to serve, warm the cakes gently in a low oven for 8-10 minutes or place in a microwave on high for 1 minute, covered.

To serve, drizzle a teaspoon of honey in a swirl or zigzag pattern on each plate. Place a cake on one side of each plate and a serving of cream on the other.

Making Beeswax Candles

It used to be believed that because bees left the Garden of Eden after the Fall, they were blessed by God, and it was therefore essential for candles that were used whenever the Catholic mass was celebrated to be made of beeswax. As beeswax is an expensive commodity, economic necessity now dictates that candles used in religious ceremonies need contain only 25 percent beeswax.

The candles are traditionally made by the dipping method: melt the wax gently in a tall, narrow container and then dip the wick quickly in and out until it is coated with wax. Pull it straight and repeat the process until the candle is the required thickness. Alternatively, if you have a suitable mold, you can pour the melted wax over the wick, again making sure the wick is straight. If you want your candles to have a honeycomb texture, you can make them simply and easily by rolling up purchased beeswax sheets.

WHOLE PEARS BAKED
en papillote

Subtly flavored with acacia honey and a hint of aniseed provided by star anise, these pears are individually baked whole *en papillote*, a method of neatly cooking food in its own juices. In this recipe, four rectangles of baking paper, each 16x18inches, are required plus lengths of string to secure the packages.

SERVES 4

4 pears with stems (about 7oz), peeled	*4 star anise*
	8 cloves
4tbsp acacia honey	*1tbsp pear liqueur*
2oz crystallized ginger, cut into strips	*½ cup crème fraîche*

Heat the oven to 375°F. Cut 4 rectangles of baking paper 16x18 inches and 4 pieces of string 10 inches long.

Pour the honey into a shallow dish and roll each pear in the honey to coat it, then lay it in the center of a paper rectangle. Sprinkle with the ginger and place 1 star anise and 2 cloves around the base of each pear.

Mix the remaining honey with the pear liqueur and drizzle evenly over the pears.

Bring the paper up loosely around each pear and tie at the top with the string to form a package. Place them on a baking sheet and bake for 15 minutes. Remove the packages from the oven, untie each one in turn, turn the pear over, and tie up once more. Return the pears to the oven and bake for 15-20 minutes until the pears are tender.

Place each package on a plate for each guest to unwrap and serve accompanied by a dish of crème fraîche.

BAKED CUSTARD HONEYPOTS

Ideal for a special occasion, these velvety, smooth old-fashioned custards are made with lavender honey rather than sugar. They can be made in advance and chilled overnight, ready to serve the next day.

SERVES 4

5½tbsp lavender honey	*only, beaten together*
1¼ cups whole milk	*¾ cup whipped cream to serve*
⅛ cup heavy cream	*8 crystallized violets for*
1 vanilla pod, split in half	*decoration*
4 eggs, 2 whole and 2 yolks	

Spoon 3 teaspoons of warmed honey into each of 4 half cup dishes, turning them so that the bottoms and sides are coated. Place the dishes immediately in the freezer for 30-40 minutes to set.

Heat the oven to 350°F.

Pour the milk into a saucepan, add the cream and vanilla pod, and bring to a boil. Remove from the heat, add the remainder of the honey, and leave to stand for a few minutes so the vanilla infuses in the milk. When the milk is lukewarm, remove the vanilla pod, scraping it with a knife to make sure all the vanilla is in the mixture. Stir the beaten eggs into the milk, mixing well.

Remove the dishes from the freezer and divide the custard mixture among them. Place the dishes in a *bain-marie* or deep baking tray and add cold water until it reaches halfway up the molds. Place in the oven and bake for 35-40 minutes until golden brown on top and an inserted skewer or sharp knife is clean when removed.

To serve, place each dish on an individual plate, spoon a portion of whipped cream on the side, and decorate with 2 crystallized violets per person.

Individual Honey Soufflés

Flavored with orange blossom honey, these light, fluffy soufflés are impressively high. For the best result, use a copper bowl and a hand beater to achieve the greatest volume possible from the egg whites.

SERVES 4

melted butter for greasing	*3tbsp orange-flavored liqueur*
½ cup superfine sugar	*pinch of salt*
6 eggs, separated and at room temperature, 4 yolks and 6 whites only	*2oz crystallized orange rind in strips*
2tbsp orange blossom honey	*½ cup extra thick heavy cream to serve*

Heat the oven to 400°F. Grease 4 high-sided 4-inch soufflé dishes with melted butter and sprinkle 1 teaspoon of sugar into each, rolling it around to coat the inside evenly.

In a large bowl, beat the 4 egg yolks with the remainder of the sugar until they are thick, creamy, and pale. Continue beating and gradually drizzle in the honey in a constant stream, then pour in the orange-flavored liqueur in the same way.

Place the egg whites in a copper bowl or a very clean ceramic bowl, add a pinch of salt, and beat until stiff and forming firm peaks. Using a metal spoon, gently fold the beaten egg whites into the egg yolk mixture. Spoon the mixture immediately into the soufflé dishes. Using the point of a sharp knife, draw a circle on the surface of the mixture, about 1 inch inside the rim of each dish; this will make the soufflé rise in two tiers.

Place the dishes on the bottom shelf of the oven, making sure there is enough room for the soufflés to rise, and bake for 10-12 minutes until rich golden brown on top.

Serve immediately with a serving of extra thick cream on the side.

Tanging

Within living memory, "tanging," or loud banging on metal objects, was thought to make a swarm of bees settle. According to the advice given in Tusser Redivivus, *published in 1744, an updated edition of Thomas Tusser's* Five Hundred Points of Good Husbandry, *originally published in 1573: "The tinkling after them with a warming pan, frying pan, kettle, is of good use to let the neighbours know you have a swarm in the air, which you claim whenever it lights." The act of tanging gave the beekeeper the right to trespass on another's land while chasing a swarm.*

Honey Packaging

There have never been many large commercial food producers in the honey business, but rather individuals or small associations of beekeepers. But because, or in spite, of this, there is a wealth of beautiful labels and packaging from the end of the last century to the present day. Generally using all the references of flowers, bees, and beekeeping, the designs are often colorful, unusual, and very distinctive. Today there are fewer interesting labels as more and more honey is bought from supermarkets with own-brand labeling, but search out a pot of honey from a small producer and chances are it will be as pretty as pots used to be. Country cottages, apple blossom or heather, straw skeps, and rustic gates all feature strongly, and somehow they always look just right.

3. *Beekeepers' associations have always been important to the marketing of honey, which is mostly produced on a small scale. Here they are selling heather honey with a picture of a bee collecting from this typically Scottish flower.*

1. *The straw bee skep appears time and time again on honey labels and advertising. It offers a safe and natural image. Interestingly, this honey has been packaged and sold by a pharmacist, so perhaps he bought in honey from local beekeepers in the area.*

2. *Wonderful artwork done for a wraparound label for a honey jar. Bees, butterflies, and apple blossom join with St. George and the Dragon, and strong typography, to produce a very decorative result.*

4. *"Make a bee-line for Be-ze-be"* seems to have been an attempt in the 1930s to up-date the image of honey. This stylish poster of the period is marketing honey as an up-to-the-minute breakfast food.

5. *The bees that made this honey would have had the full range of flowers from the Pyrenees from which to gather nectar.*

6. *This British importer obviously felt that Californian honey was superior to home-produced varieties.*

7. *Australia is one of the biggest exporters of honey and has long been in the business of marketing it all over the world. This impressive label suggests a confident commerciality.*

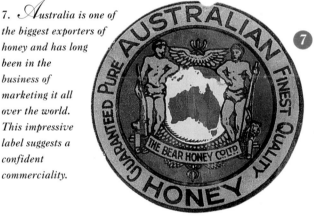

8. *There is no arguing with the message on this French honey label. It is simply the best of the harvest. When this was made, there was little use for weights and measures and accurate labeling.*

9. *Some slightly daring claims on this packaging for section-comb honey from Russells. These days the wording would have to be more bland – and so might the product.*

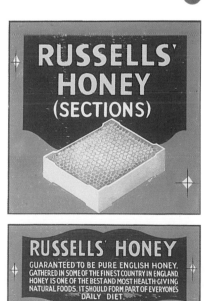

CHAPTER FIVE

CAKES AND COOKIES

In addition to being a sweetener, honey brings its own unique tastes and savors to food. In cakes and cookies, honey's wonderfully subtle flavors really come into their own. Orange blossom honey in a Middle Eastern-inspired layered pastry and rich dark chestnut honey in a light-as-air yellow cake are just two examples: subtle use of honey can create culinary perfection.

CAKES AND COOKIES

Homemade cakes and cookies, still warm from the oven, are always a treat, but only honey can impart that all-important richness, subtlety of flavor, and moistness. Wild honey was the staple sweetener long before cane and beet sugar, but it was never plentiful. So cakes and cookies were a rare treat. Honey has provided sweetness, preservative qualities, and moisture to an enormous variety of gingerbread recipes throughout Europe since medieval times. The Polish city of Torun, on the main spice route from the East and with its thriving honey industry, became an important center for gingerbread. And as Hansel and Gretel found out when they ventured into the woods, the sweet tang of gingerbread is impossible to resist.

A French manuscript, sixteenth century.

111

APPLE *and* CINNAMON CAKE

The aroma of baked apple and cinnamon, enhanced by a generous amount of comb honey, makes this moist, spiced upside-down cake irresistible – just right for an after-school snack, or indeed at any time of the day.

MAKES AN 8-INCH CAKE

butter for greasing
3½tsp ground cinnamon
½ cup superfine sugar
2 red eating apples such as
 Cox's Orange Pippins,
 peeled, cored and thinly
 sliced

2 cups self-rising flour
1½ sticks butter
3oz comb honey
3 eggs, beaten and at room
 temperature
½ cup milk

Heat the oven to 350°F.

Grease a deep 8-inch diameter cake pan with melted butter. Mix ½ teaspoon of the cinnamon with 1 tablespoon of the sugar and sprinkle over the base of the pan. Line the base of the pan with the apple slices, overlapping them so that there are no gaps for the cake mixture to leak through. Sift the flour with the remainder of the cinnamon into a bowl. Set aside.

Cream the butter with the remainder of the sugar until the mixture is light and fluffy. Gradually pour in the honey in a constant stream, beating continuously, and then add the beaten eggs gradually; the mixture will curdle if you add them all at once. Add 2 tablespoons of flour at a time to the creamed mixture, folding with a large metal spoon, then pouring in a little milk. Continue folding in, alternating the flour with the milk and finishing off with flour.

Pour the mixture into the greased cake pan and bake for 40-45 minutes, until an inserted skewer or pointed knife comes out clean. Allow to cool for 15-20 minutes, then turn the cake out onto a cooling rack. The apples should be caramelized and the cake a rich golden brown.

HONEYCOMB

Comfortingly sweet, this crunchy aerated caramel is made in a slab, rather like old-fashioned toffees were, then broken up into irregular pieces revealing its honeycomb-like structure. Good on its own, it is even more enjoyable served with rich vanilla ice cream. Store the "honeycomb" in an airtight container in the refrigerator; air softens the candy.

MAKES ONE 7X12-INCH SLAB

butter for greasing
3tbsp light-colored honey
¾ cup superfine sugar
1tbsp light corn syrup
1¾tsp baking soda

Line a shallow 7 x 12-inch sandwich tin with foil greased with butter.

Put the honey, sugar, and corn syrup in a high-sided saucepan, and pour in 3 tablespoons of water; you will need a pan deep enough to contain the liquid when the baking soda is added, as this will make the syrup foam and increase in volume. Place over a low heat until the sugar is fully dissolved; the sugar must be completely dissolved at this stage to prevent it from crystallizing when the syrup is brought to a boil.

Bring the syrup to a boil and then simmer until it reaches 300°F, the hard crack stage; beyond this stage the sugar syrup will burn. If you do not have a sugar thermometer, you can test whether the syrup is ready. Using a clean teaspoon, take a little syrup and drop it into a bowl of ice-cold water. Remove the syrup and bend it. If it snaps instead of bending, it has reached the hard crack stage.

Remove the saucepan immediately from the heat and stir in the baking soda. Pour the syrup into the greased baking pan and leave it for about 1 hour to set. Once set, crack the "honeycomb" into pieces with the back of a knife.

Bees cluster around a honeycomb, busily producing honey in its purest form. The sophisticated hexagonal structure of the comb is unique in nature.

TURKISH DELIGHT

Authentic Turkish Delight is a delicate, exotic, rosewater-scented confection that will turn anyone trying it for the first time into an immediate addict. To make a pretty present, wrap it in cellophane, with a few rose petals if you like, and tie it up with ribbon in various shades of pink.

MAKES 25 SQUARES

5½oz very light-colored honey	*½ cup powdered sugar*
1¼ cups sugar	*2tbsp cornstarch*
1tbsp rosewater	*½ cup filberts*
2tbsp gelatin	*rose petals for decoration*
2 or more drops red food coloring	

Pour ¾ cup water into a deep-sided saucepan; when the gelatin is added later, the syrup will foam and increase in volume. Add the honey and sugar and stir over a low heat until the sugar is fully dissolved. Then bring to a boil, gently skimming off any froth with a clean metal spoon without disturbing the syrup.

Boil the syrup rapidly for about 15-20 minutes until it reaches 240°F, the soft ball stage. If you do not own a sugar thermometer, you can test whether the syrup is ready. Using a clean teaspoon, drop a little syrup into a bowl of ice-cold water and mold the syrup into a ball. If the syrup holds its shape, it has reached the soft ball stage.

While the syrup is boiling, place the rosewater in a small bowl with 3 tablespoons of hot, but not boiling, water. Sprinkle on the gelatin and stir rapidly with a fork until nearly dissolved. Place the bowl of gelatin in a large bowl of boiling water to keep the gelatin liquid until needed.

When the syrup has reached the soft ball stage, remove from the heat and add the gelatin solution with 2 or more drops of food coloring to achieve the desired shade of pink.

Rinse an 8-inch square or similar pan under water, to prevent sticking. Pour in the syrup and skim the top to make it perfectly clear. Leave overnight to set.

Using a sharp knife dipped in warm water, cut the Turkish Delight into 1½-inch squares. Mix the powdered sugar and cornstarch together and sprinkle over a tray. Toss the Turkish Delight squares in this and serve on a plate sprinkled with filberts and decorated with rose petals.

SPICE BREAD

Spice bread, also known as *pain d'épice*, has a long tradition in many European countries, where it is often molded into a variety of shapes and elaborately decorated. Although strictly a bread, its dependence on honey and sweet spices places it firmly in the cake category. It is particularly good with a glass of Mulled Cider (page 124).

MAKES 1 LOAF OR SHAPE

2¾ cups all-purpose flour   *¼tsp ground cinnamon*
14oz any dark-colored honey   *1tsp ground ginger*
3tsp baking powder   *1tbsp milk for glazing*
¼tsp ground cloves

Sift the flour into a heatproof bowl and make a well in the center. Pour the honey into a small saucepan and bring it to a boil, skimming off any foam with a clean metal spoon. Pour the hot honey into the flour, mixing it to form a thick, moist paste. Place the paste on greased film, wrap tightly and leave to rest at room temperature for 1-1½ hours.

Forty minutes into the resting time, heat the oven to 375°F. When this time is over, unwrap the rested paste which should now feel more like a dough. Sprinkle the baking powder onto a countertop and position the paste on it. Knead for 3-4 minutes until all the baking powder is mixed in. Repeat this procedure with the cloves, cinnamon, and ginger, then knead for a further 3-4 minutes.

Press the mixture into a greased loaf pan or gingerbread mold, or fashion it into a flattened heart shape. Bake for 20-25 minutes until it is golden brown and sounds hollow when tapped on the top; the cooking time will depend on the depth of the mold or pan, so you may need to allow an extra 5-8 minutes for the mixture to be cooked right through.

Turn off the oven and remove the spiced bread. Brush it with milk and return it to the warm oven for 3-4 minutes to set a glaze on the bread. Allow the bread to cool before serving.

LIGHT HONEY CAKE *with* MARSCAPONE

The nutty, slightly caramel flavor of chestnut honey permeates this tall, divinely light cake as well as its filling and topping of marscapone, a rich Italian cream cheese.

MAKES AN 8-INCH CAKE

butter for greasing	2tsp butter melted
4 eggs, at room temperature	in 2tbsp hot water
½ cup superfine sugar	TOPPING
3oz chestnut honey	1lb marscapone
1¼ cups self-rising flour	2½tbsp chestnut honey

Heat the oven to 350°F. Grease an 8-inch diameter and 3¼-inch deep cake pan with butter.

Beat the eggs and sugar together in a large bowl until doubled in volume and the sugar is dissolved. Continue beating and slowly pour in the honey in a continuous stream.

Sift the flour twice, then sift again into the egg and honey mixture. Fold in quickly with a metal spoon, then fold in the butter and hot water.

Pour the mixture into the cake pan. Bake for 20-25 minutes until the cake is a rich golden brown and an inserted skewer or pointed knife comes out clean. Allow to cool for 5-8 minutes before turning out onto a cooling rack.

To make the topping, mix the marscapone and 2 tablespoons of chestnut honey together.

When the cake is cool, slice it in half horizontally with a bread knife. Place the base on a serving plate and spread it with half of the marscapone mixture. Replace the top and spread with the remainder of the mixture. To decorate, drizzle the remaining honey over the top to create swirls.

HONEY *and* PECAN MUFFINS

Freshly baked muffins conjure up comforting images of good old-fashioned home cooking and these, sweetened with acacia honey and stuffed with pecans, do not disappoint.

MAKES 12 SMALL MUFFINS

2tbsp melted butter, plus extra for greasing	1 cup whole-wheat self-rising flour
1 egg, at room temperature	½ cup pecans, roughly chopped
1½tbsp acacia honey	1tsp ground cinnamon
⅝ cup whole milk	

Heat the oven to 400°F. Brush a 12-cup muffin pan with melted butter.

Beat the egg with the honey, then pour in the milk and melted butter and mix. Pour the mixture into a large measuring cup.

Place the whole-wheat self-rising flour, pecans, and cinnamon into a large bowl. Make a well in the center and gradually pour in the egg mixture, stirring quickly with a spoon about 10-12 times only, so that the batter is not overworked; it does not matter if the mixture is slightly lumpy.

Put the batter into the muffin cups using a spoon and gently pushing the batter off the spoon in one movement using a spatula; any topping-up would result in the muffins not rising successfully. Place in the oven and cook for 15-20 minutes until risen and golden brown and an inserted skewer or pointed knife comes out clean.

Serve the muffins hot with lashings of sweet butter.

ALMOND *and* PINE NUT BAKLAVA

Baklava are the traditional sweetmeats of the Middle East. Made in the same time-honored way for centuries, they comprise wedges of phyllo pastry soaked in a heady honey syrup and alternated with layers of chopped, spiced exotic nuts. Although they appear complicated, they are quite straightforward to make.

MAKES 24 PIECES

6tbsp butter, melted	*20 sheets phyllo pastry (about*
½ cup flaked almonds	*12oz)*
¼ cup pine nuts	SYRUP
⅓ cup macadamia nuts	*9oz orange blossom honey*
3tsp ground cinnamon	*2tsp orange flower water*
⅜ cup superfine sugar	

Heat the oven to 350°F. Grease a 7 x 12-inch loaf pan with some of the butter.

Finely chop the almonds, pine nuts, and macadamia nuts in a food processor or by hand. Mix the chopped nuts with the cinnamon and sugar.

To keep the phyllo moist while working, cover it with a damp, but not wet, dishtowel. Cut the pastry sheets to fit the pan. Place one sheet of pastry in the pan, then brush it with the melted butter. Place another sheet in the pan and repeat the process until 5 sheets are in the pan. Spread one third of the nut mixture over the pastry. Layer with 5 more sheets, brushing each with butter, then spread another third of the mixture over them. Repeat with 5 more sheets and spread these with the remainder of the nut mixture. Top with 5 more layers of buttered pastry.

Using a sharp pointed knife, score the top layers of pastry on the diagonal about 1½ inches apart, then again in the opposite direction to make diamond shapes. Place in the oven and bake for 45-50 minutes until golden brown.

Make the syrup a few minutes before the baklava has finished cooking. Pour the honey and the orange flower water into a saucepan with 4 tablespoons of water, heat for 2-3 minutes until hot and remove from the heat.

As soon as the baklava is cooked, remove from the oven and pour the hot syrup over it. Allow to cool before cutting out the diamond shapes and serving.

119

Buzzing Bees

"There was an old man in a tree,
Who was horribly bored by a bee;
When they said, 'Does it buzz?'
He replied, 'Yes, it does!
It's a regular brute of a bee!'"

BOOK OF NONSENSE,
EDWARD LEAR, 1812–88

Skeps

The most popular image associated with beehives is that of the
traditional straw skep, one of the earliest forms of man-made hives.
However, the design created problems for the
beekeeper. The bees filled up the entire inside of
the skep with their wax comb, so the workers
were not separated in any way from the queen
and her attendant drones. Thus, in order to
retrieve his honey, the beekeeper had to kill his
bees. The design was improved in Medieval
times: a separate chamber, called an "eke,"
with the same diameter as the skep and about
4 inches high, was placed under the skep. The
bees built a new comb in the eke, which could
be easily extracted as a unit without
disturbing the bees too much, particularly the
all-important queen.
The honey was then sliced off with a knife
and the eke replaced to be used once more.

120

GREEK HONEYED DOUGHNUTS

MAKES 10 DOUGHNUTS

1½ cups all-purpose flour
1tsp easy-bake yeast
2tsp ground cinnamon
¼tsp salt
3tbsp milk, warmed
1 egg, beaten
4 cups sunflower oil for
*   frying*

½ cup chopped brazil nuts
SYRUP
6oz Greek mountain honey or
*   other clear*
*   dark honey*
1 cinnamon stick
1tbsp freshly squeezed
*   orange juice*

Place the flour, yeast, cinnamon, and salt in a bowl, then make a well in the center. Mix the warm milk with 6 tablespoons of warm water and pour into the well. Carefully stir the liquid with a spoon until the flour gradually falls in from the sides and is incorporated to form a smooth batter. Add the beaten egg and continue to beat until large air bubbles begin to appear, then set aside.

To make the syrup, place all the ingredients in a saucepan and heat gently for 3-4 minutes until slightly syrupy. Set aside.

In a deep fryer or deep-sided saucepan, heat the oil until the temperature reaches 350-375°F; if you do not own a thermometer, drop in a piece of bread – if it browns, the oil is ready. Gently lower a spoonful of the batter into the oil, pushing it off the spoon with another spoon or spatula so the shape is nicely formed and no bits of batter go astray. Fry the doughnuts in batches of 3 or 4 until they are golden-brown, removing them with a slotted spoon and placing them on a layer of paper towels to drain.

Put the doughnuts in a dish with raised sides and pour on the honey syrup. Leave for 10-15 minutes, then turn them and leave for another 10 minutes until the syrup is absorbed.

To serve the doughnuts, reheat them in a microwave oven set on high for 10-15 seconds or in a warm oven for 5 minutes. Serve sprinkled with the chopped brazil nuts.

Greek doughnuts, known as *loukmades*, are round, do not have a hole, and are wickedly saturated with honey syrup. Although not essential, the Greek mountain honey used here gives them an authentic touch.

121

Afternoon Tea

" . . . the ample charms of a genuine Dutch country tea table, in the sumptuous time of autumn. Such heaped-up platters of cakes of various and almost indescribable kinds . . . There was the doughty doughnut, the tenderer oly koek, and the crisp and crumbling cruller; sweet cakes and shortcakes, ginger cakes and honey cakes . . . And then there were apple pies and peach pies and pumpkin pies; beside slices of ham and smoked beef; and moreover delectable dishes of preserved plums, and peaches, and pears, and quinces . . . together with bowls of milk and cream, all mingled higgledy-piggledy . . . with the motherly teapot sending up its clouds of vapor from the midst."

THE LEGEND OF SLEEPY HOLLOW,
WASHINGTON IRVING, 1783–1859

122

CREAMY HONEY FUDGE

Heavenly smooth and chewy, this fudge evokes memories of crinkly toffee papers, giant candy jars, and childhood longings in the corner store. To achieve the right texture, you will need to cook the fudge at a precise temperature, making a sugar thermometer essential.

MAKES 36 SQUARES

10oz creamy set honey
1 cup superfine sugar
¾ cup light cream

3tbsp butter, plus extra for greasing

Place the honey, sugar, and cream in a saucepan and stir over a low heat until the sugar is completely dissolved; it is essential that the sugar does this to prevent it from crystallizing when the syrup is brought to a boil. Bring to a boil and when the temperature reaches 240°F, then boil rapidly at exactly this temperature for 12-15 minutes.

Remove from the heat and add the butter. Allow to cool to 100°F, then pour into a bowl and beat with a wooden spoon for about 5 minutes until the fudge is creamy and thick; this is hard work, but important to obtain the correct texture.

Spoon the fudge mixture into a greased 7 x 12-inch baking pan and leave for about 2-3 hours to set.

When set, cut the fudge into 1-inch squares with a knife dipped in cold water.

PEANUT BUTTER *and* HONEY COOKIES

Crisp and light, these cookies are good served with coffee or the Hot Honeyed Cardamom Milk drink on page 124.

MAKES 24-26 COOKIES

1 stick butter

¼ cup light brown sugar plus extra for dusting

4oz Australian honey

1 egg, at room temperature

½ cup extra crunchy peanut butter

1 cup self-rising flour

1 cup all-purpose flour

Heat the oven to 350°F. Line a baking sheet with baking parchment or a baking roll.

In a large bowl, cream the butter with the sugar until light and fluffy. Slowly pour in the honey, beating continuously. Beat in the egg and peanut butter and mix well. Using a large metal spoon, fold in the self-rising and the all-purpose flours, incorporating all the flour.

With floured hands, roll the mixture into walnut-sized balls and place on the baking sheet, spaced well apart as they will spread when baked. With a fork dipped in flour, make an impression and flatten each ball. Place in the center of the oven and bake for 10-12 minutes, turning the tray halfway through to cook the cookies evenly.

Remove the cookies from the oven and carefully slide the baking parchment off the tray and onto a cooling rack to prevent the cookies from cooking any more. Allow to cool until firm and crunchy, then serve.

Drinks

Throughout the centuries honey has been an essential ingredient in many drinks, from African beer and monastic liqueurs such as Benedictine, to traditional honey-whiskey-lemon hot toddy.

BEE STING

Serve this potent cocktail as a stimulating pre-dinner drink or at a party.

MAKES 2½ CUPS
2 lemons, juice only
2½tbsp orange blossom honey
½ cup whiskey
1 egg, white only
4 ice cubes
DECORATION
1 lemon, peel only
3½tbsp superfine sugar, plus extra for sprinkling

To make the decoration, peel a long strip of skin from the lemon using a vegetable peeler and slice it lengthwise to make four long, thin twists about 2 inches wide.

Place the sugar in a saucepan with 3 tablespoons of water and heat gently until the sugar is dissolved. Add the lemon twists and simmer for about 7-8 minutes. Remove the twists from the sugar syrup and lay them on baking paper. Sprinkle with sugar.

Place all the cocktail ingredients in a food processor. Blend until frothy and the ice cubes are crushed.

Serve in stem glasses, each decorated with a lemon twist.

HOT HONEYED CARDAMON MILK

Taken as a bedtime drink, especially several nights in a row, this soothing beverage should encourage uninterrupted slumber and sweet dreams. The cardamom pods are pierced to allow their aromatic flavor to infuse the milk.

MAKES 3 CUPS
12 cardamom pods
1¼ tbsp clear honey
3 cups whole milk

Pierce 10 of the cardamom pods with a skewer or sharp, pointed knife. Break open the 2 remaining pods, discard the skins, and crush the seeds into a fine powder using a mortar and pestle.

Melt the honey in a saucepan. Add the cardamom pods and crushed seeds and stir for 1-2 minutes over a low heat.

Pour in the milk and heat gently until hot. Leave on a low heat for 8-10 minutes to allow the cardamom flavor to diffuse through the milk. Strain the milk through fine mesh into a pitcher and pour into four mugs.

MULLED CIDER

Sweetened with fragrant Greek mountain honey, this gently warmed spiced cider will bring cheer to a winter's day or make a change from eggnog at a Christmas party.

MAKES 4 CUPS
2tbsp Greek mountain honey
2in piece cinnamon stick
6 cloves
1 whole nutmeg, grated roughly on the sides
1 curl mace
½ candied orange, peel only
4 cups strong dry cider

Place the honey, cinnamon stick, cloves, nutmeg, mace, and candied orange peel in a saucepan and simmer gently for 1-2 minutes to release the flavors of the spices.

Pour in the cider and warm over a low heat for 8-10 minutes, but do not allow to boil.

Remove the saucepan from the heat and strain the mulled cider into four good-sized glasses. Slice the candied orange peel into four strips and place one in each glass.

Honey, Banana, and Yogurt Smoothie

Wholesome enough for a high-speed breakfast, this deliciously healthy drink is also a refreshing daytime energizer. Serve it sprinkled, if you wish, with bran for extra fiber.

MAKES 4 CUPS

2tbsp clover honey
3tbsp thick plain yogurt
2 cups milk
2 bananas, roughly chopped
2tsp bran, optional

Place all the ingredients in a food processor and blend until smooth. Place in the freezer and chill for 30 minutes.

Sparkling Honey, Ginger, and White Wine Cup

Made with traditional ginger ale and honey, this delectable drink is just right for a hot, sunny day.

MAKES 4 CUPS

2 cups dry or medium dry white wine
1¼tbsp orange blossom honey, warmed
2 cups traditional ginger ale
1oz crystallized ginger, cut into strips
    for decoration

Mix a little of the white wine with the warmed honey in a large pitcher, and beat together until the honey is dissolved.

Gradually pour in the rest of the white wine and then the ginger ale. Mix well.

Place a strip of crystallized ginger in each stem glass, then fill.

Honey Egg Nog

Sweetened by honey and fortified with brandy, this is a good, old-fashioned nourishing cold excluder as enjoyed by our ancestors.

MAKES 4 CUPS

4 eggs, separated
1½tbsp clear honey
2¼ cups skimmed or whole milk
3tbsp brandy
¼tsp ground nutmeg
¼tsp ground cinnamon

Whip the egg yolks and honey until frothy and turning pale yellow.

Heat the milk in a medium-sized saucepan until bubbles are just forming around the edges of the saucepan.

Meanwhile, beat the egg whites until frothy and just forming soft peaks. Set aside.

Pour the warmed milk and the brandy into the bowl containing the egg yolk mixture, beating constantly until blended. Next, fold in the egg whites using a large metal spoon.

Serve immediately in mugs or thick-sided goblets, sprinkled with the ground nutmeg and cinnamon.

General Index

INDEX *of* RECIPES

ACKNOWLEDGEMENTS

Key: (*a*) above (*b*) below, *c* centre, *l* left, *r* right.
I B R A: International Bee Research Association
H and N H P: Heritage and Natural History Photography

Page *6 l* Roger-Viollet; *7 a* & *br* Robert Opie; *8a* M S Ashmole 1423 Bodleian
Library, University of Oxford; *8b* Ron and Christine Foord; *9a* Andrew
Henley/Biofotos; *10* Ann Ronan at Image Select; *11a* Mansell Collection;
11b & *12a* H and N H P; *12b* & *13b* Ann Ronan at Image Select;
13 cl & *cr* H and N H P; *14a* & *bl* Ann Ronan at Image Select, *14br* & *15al*
Roger-Viollet; *15 ar, bl, br* & *17l* H and N H P; *19ar* Sipa/Rex Features,
*19b*l Billie Love Historical Collection; *20l* C M Dixon, *20r* H and N H P,
20b Mansell Collection; *21* C M Dixon; *22al* & *bl* e.t. archive; *23al* M S Auct
F.4.15, *23bl* M S Douce 88 f.III v & *23r* Bodleian Library, University of
Oxford; *24a* & *b* Ann Ronan at Image Select; *25a* & *br* Roger-Viollet,
25bl H and N H P; *26a* & *27a* Mansell Collection, *27b* Natural Food
Company; *28a* Mansell Collection; *29a* Natural Food Company, *29br* Mansell
Collection; *30a* Natural Food Company, *30b, 31b* & *32a* Mansell Collection;
32l Robert Opie; *33b* Mansell Collection; *34a* Roger-Viollet; *35ar* Robert Opie,
35 br Mansell Collection; *36b* Philip and Karen Smith/Tony Stone Images;
43 Visual Arts Library; *44br* Robert Opie; *54* Harry Smith Horticultural
Collection; *55al* Christie's Images, *55ar* C M Dixon; *55b* Christie's Images;
59 Visual Arts Library; *65bl* Christie's Images; *66a* Roger-Viollet; *66b* Alain
Choisnet/Image Bank; *71* M S Bodley 264, fol. 73v Bodleian Library,
University of Oxford; *72al* & *ar* I B R A; *72b, 73al, ar* & *c* Christie's Images;
73bl, br & *cl* I B R A; *77* e.t. archive; *88-89* Ann Ronan at Image Select;
93 Visual Arts Library; *104* Ann Ronan at Image Select; *106-7* Robert Opie;
111 M S Canon, Liturg. 99. fol. 16 Bodleian Library, University of Oxford;
114b Peter Poulides/Tony Stone Images; *120a* Ann Ronan at Image Select;
120br Roger-Viollet.

All other photographs are the copyright of Quarto Publishing plc.

Quarto would like to thank Dr John B Free of Heritage and Natural History
Photography and the following who kindly provided materials and equipment
for photography: Bear Creek Woodworks, 250 Broadway, Quincy, IL 62306,
U. S. A. (shelves pp.56-7 & pp.90-1); The Canadian Honey Council, 196
Stephen Street, Richmond Hill, Ontario L4C 5P1 (honey p.37); Juliet Phillips,
Surrey (pp 16-19) and T R Tutton, Priors Leaze Cottage, Hambrook,
Chichester, West Sussex PO18 8RQ (skep p. 120).